Fun Songs for Ukulele

50 Popular Songs in Notation and Tablature, Plus Chord Charts

by Ron Middlebrook

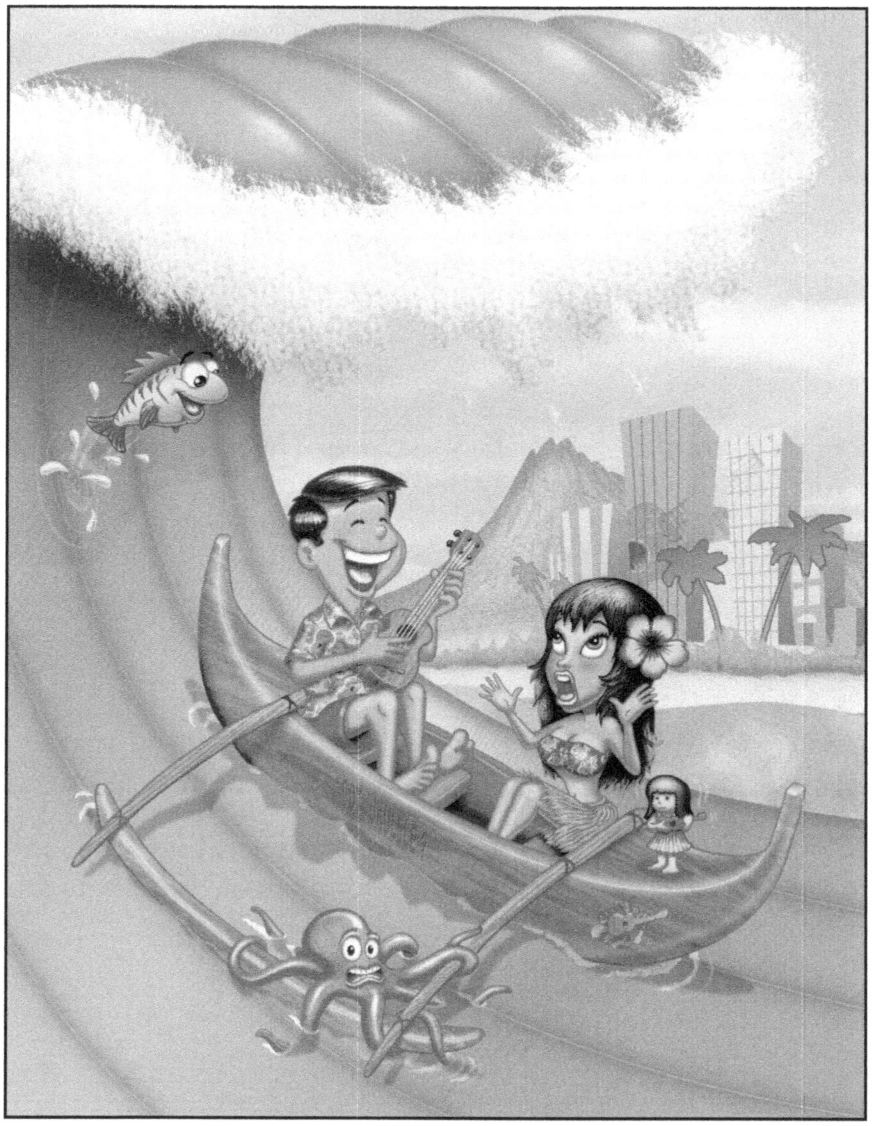

Cover Art - Eddie Young
Layout - Ken Warfield

ISBN 978-1-57424-172-3
SAN 683-8022

P.O. Box 17878 - Anaheim Hills, CA 92817

Table of Contents

Tablature

All of the music in this book is written in standard musical notation and tablature. In tab, there are 4 lines, each representing a string on the uke. Numbers are placed on the lines corresponding to the frets on which you place your fingers.

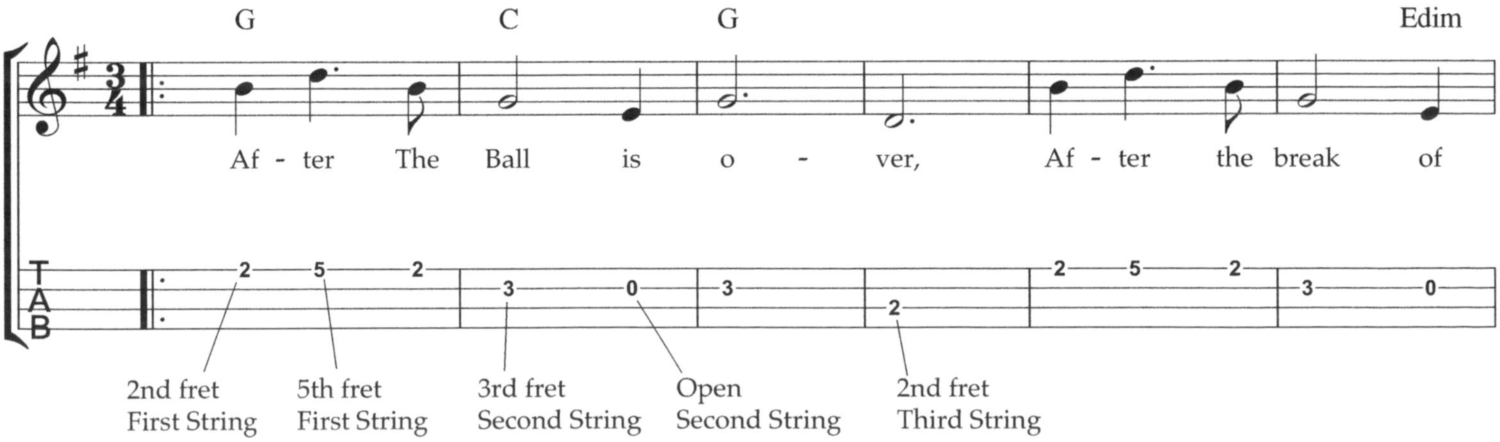

Holding the Ukulele

Keep both hands in an easy position without the slightest rigidity or strain upon any of the muscles.

The Left Hand

Place the tip of the thumb at about the center of the back of the Ukulele neck. Do not rest the neck of the Ukulele in the palm of your hand. Keep forearm and hand in an easy position. The fingers should curve naturally over the fingerboard and be able to press down lightly with the tips. Fingernails should be cut short, never allow the nails to come in contact with the strings as they have a tendency to cut them.

The Right Hand and Forearm

Let the middle of the forearm press the back edge of the ukulele to your body, holding it firmly but not too tight, so that you may be able to play either in a standing or sitting position.

Explanation of Strokes

There are many STROKES for the ukulele but the Common Stroke is the base or foundation for all.

The numerals 1,2, and 3 indicate the number of fingers used in the stroke and the U and the D indicate the up and down movements. When marked thus: 1/D means the up-stroke with one finger. When marked 3/D, it means a down stroke with three fingers.

The following strokes are suggested only, feel free to make up your own stroke to match the song.

The Common Stroke

A full round tone is best achieved by strumming the fingers at an angle to the upper part of the body of the Ukulele, this will bring the wrist directly above the sound hole.

The Stroke is made with the fore-finger of the right hand running it rapidly across all the strings with a down and up movement of the wrist, which must be perfectly free and keeping all the other fingers in readiness for another position. The down-stroke should be made squarely on the nail of the finger and the up-stroke with the fleshy part of the finger, but not on the side. There are two strokes to the beat, down and up. Make the down and up strokes even and smooth. Avoid jerkiness.

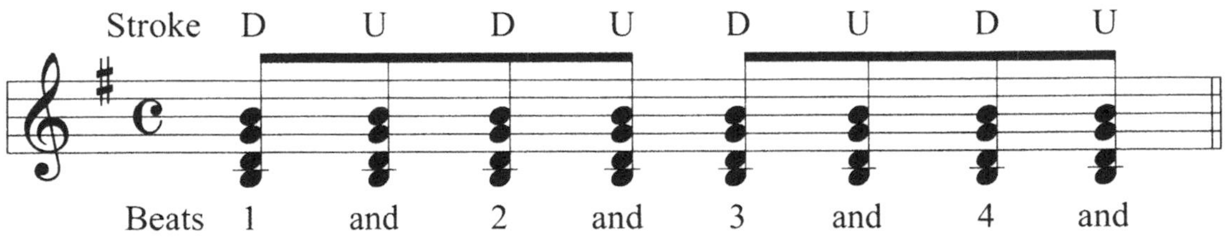

The Tremolo Stroke

This stroke is made in the same manner as the Common Stroke (down and up) but twice as fast. It must be played rapidly in order to produce a Tremolo effect.

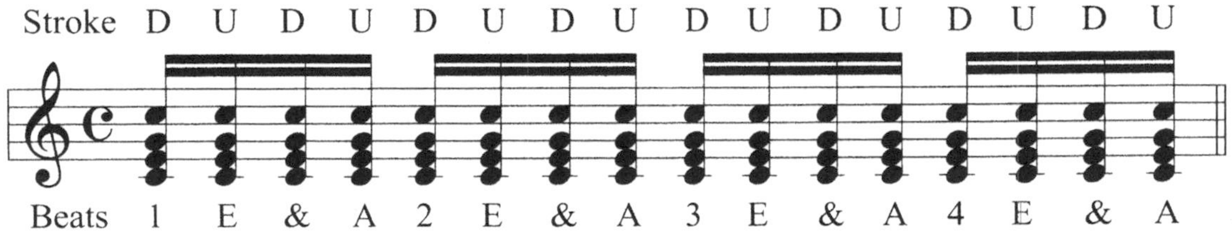

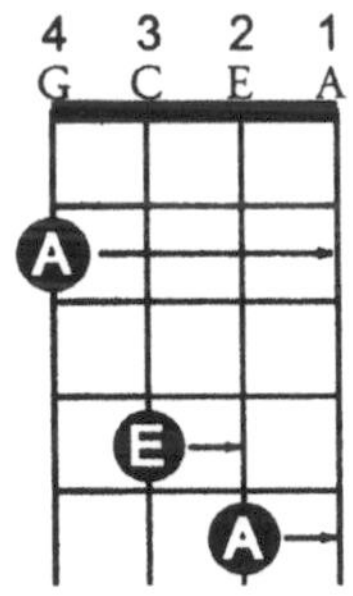

Relative Tuning

Whenever a pitch pipe, piano or another tuned ukulele is not available to you for tuning, the relative tuning method can be used. This method will allow the uke to be in tune with itself, but not necessarily in tune with any other instrument.

1. Turn the tuning peg of the 1st string (A) until it is fairly tight and produces a high tone.
2. Press the 5th fret of the 2nd string (E) and tune to <u>equal</u> the pitch of the 1st string (A).
3. Press the 4th fret of the 3rd string (C) and tune to <u>equal</u> the pitch of the 2nd string (E).
4. Press the 2nd fret of the 4th string (G) and tune to <u>equal</u> the pitch of the 1st string (A).

Ukulele Fingerboard

If you see the sharp symbol #, it means to *raise* the pitch one fret higher. The flat symbol b means to *lower* the pitch one fret back.

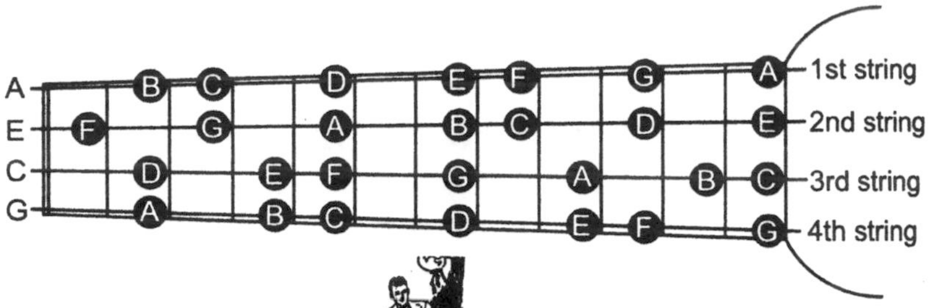

Ukulele Chords

The chord fingerings are only suggestive, you may find other fingerings that are easier.

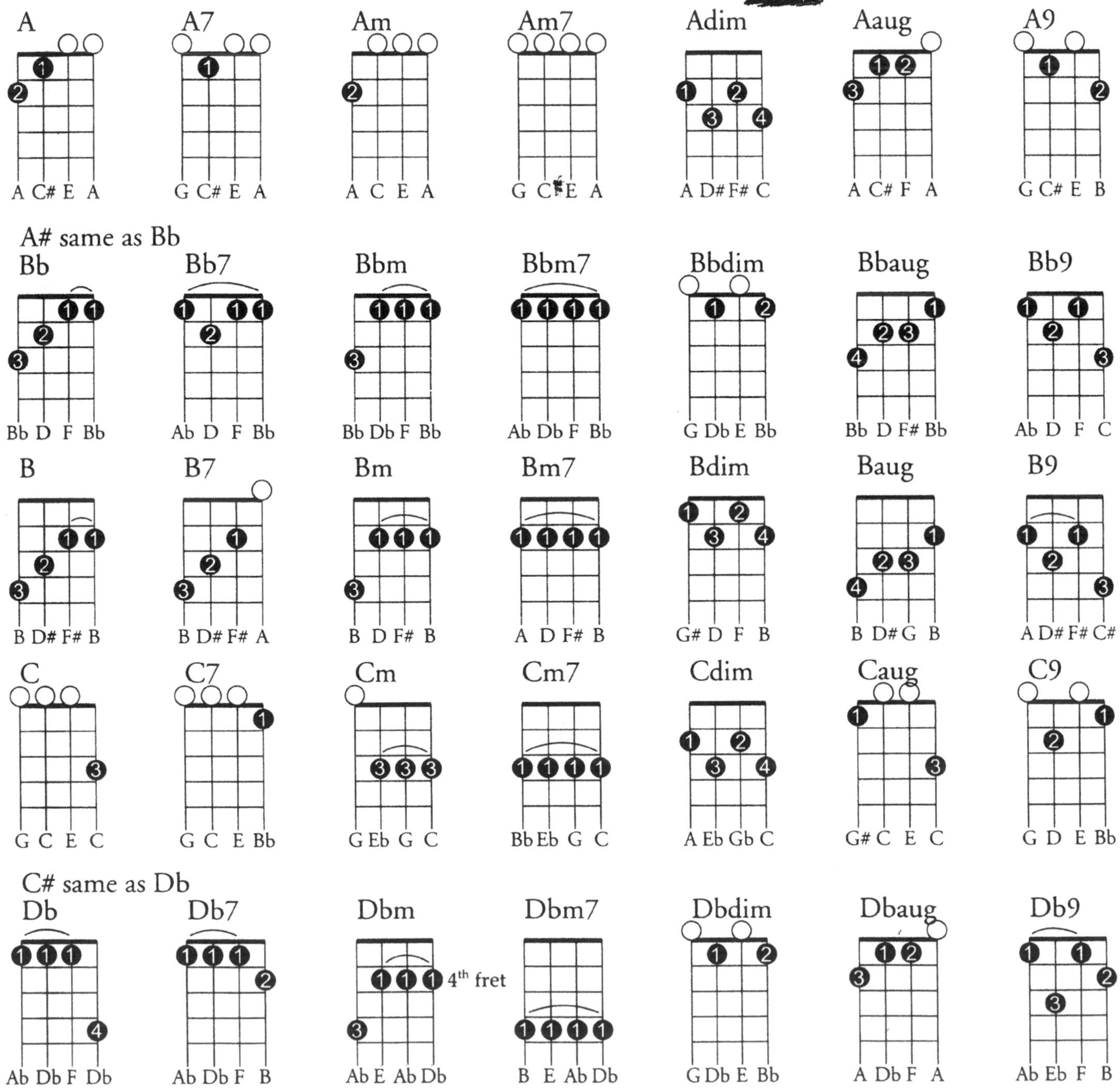

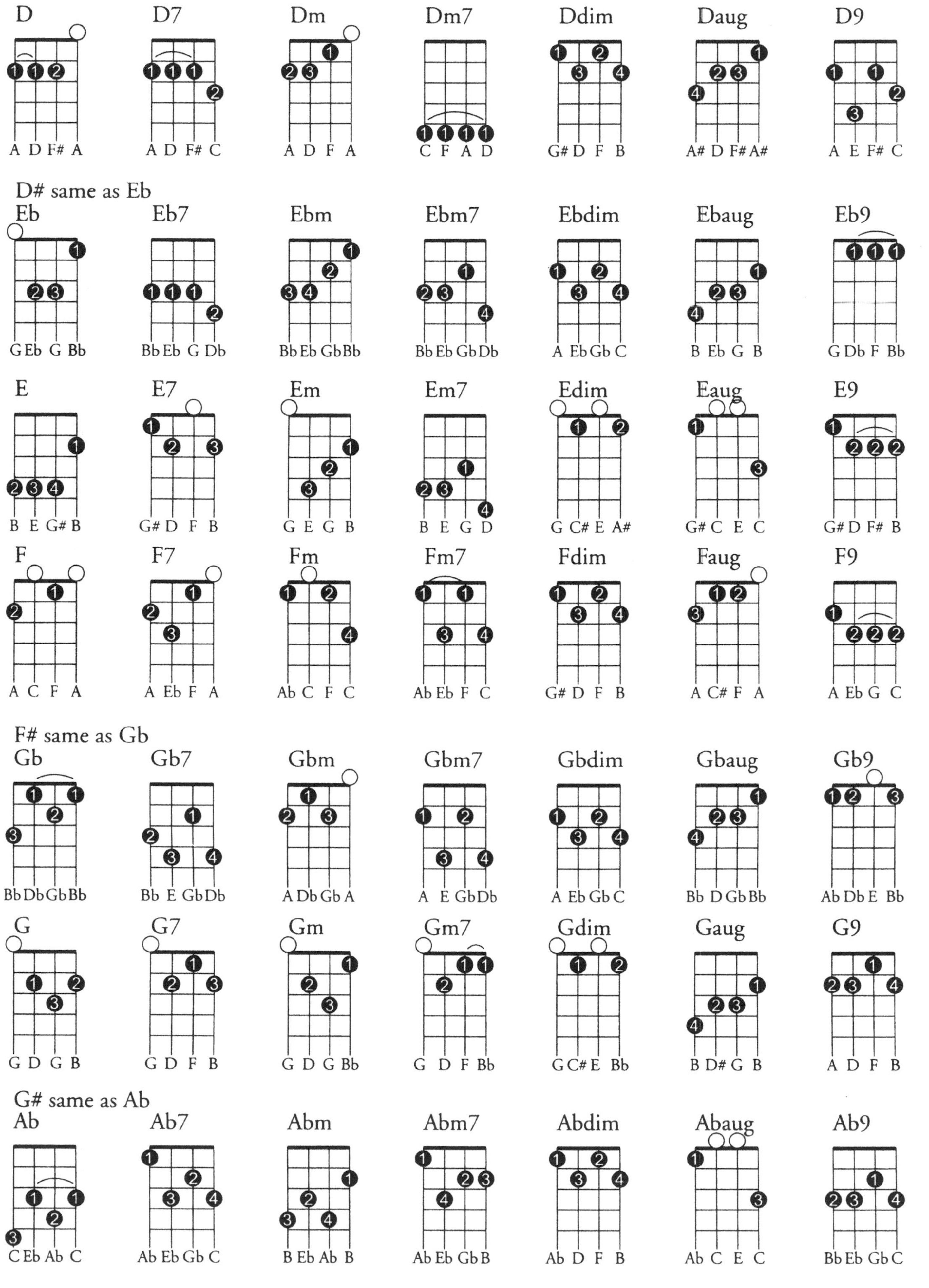
D
A D F# A
D7
A D F# C
Dm
A D F A
Dm7
C F A D
Ddim
G# D F B
Daug
A# D F# A#
D9
A E F# C
D# same as Eb
Eb
G Eb G Bb
Eb7
Bb Eb G Db
Ebm
Bb Eb Gb Bb
Ebm7
Bb Eb Gb Db
Ebdim
A Eb Gb C
Ebaug
B Eb G B
Eb9
G Db F Bb
E
B E G# B
E7
G# D F B
Em
G E G B
Em7
B E G D
Edim
G C# E A#
Eaug
G# C E C
E9
G# D F# B
F
A C F A
F7
A Eb F A
Fm
Ab C F C
Fm7
Ab Eb F C
Fdim
G# D F B
Faug
A C# F A
F9
A Eb G C
F# same as Gb
Gb
Bb Db Gb Bb
Gb7
Bb E Gb Db
Gbm
A Db Gb A
Gbm7
A E Gb Db
Gbdim
A Eb Gb C
Gbaug
Bb D Gb Bb
Gb9
Ab Db E Bb
G
G D G B
G7
G D F B
Gm
G D G Bb
Gm7
G D F Bb
Gdim
G C# E Bb
Gaug
B D# G B
G9
A D F B
G# same as Ab
Ab
C Eb Ab C
Ab7
Ab Eb Gb C
Abm
B Eb Ab B
Abm7
Ab Eb Gb B
Abdim
Ab D F B
Abaug
Ab C E C
Ab9
Bb Eb Gb C

The Aba Daba Honeymoon

By Arthur Fields and
Walter Donovan

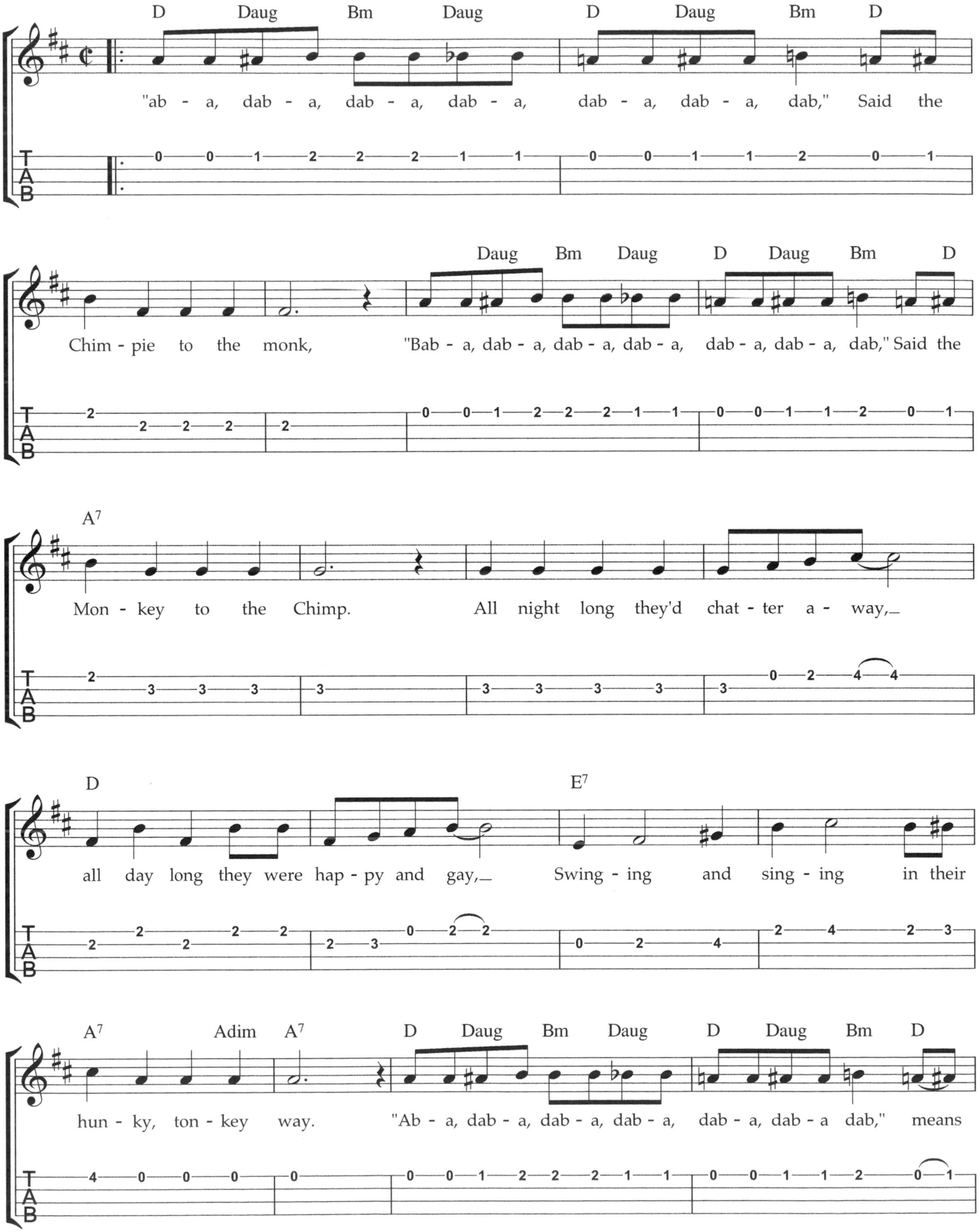
D Daug Bm Daug D Daug Bm D
"ab - a, dab - a, dab - a, dab - a, dab - a, dab - a, dab," Said the
Daug Bm Daug D Daug Bm D
Chim - pie to the monk, "Bab - a, dab - a, dab - a, dab - a, dab - a, dab - a, dab," Said the
A7
Mon - key to the Chimp. All night long they'd chat - ter a - way,
D E7
all day long they were hap - py and gay, Swing - ing and sing - ing in their
A7 Adim A7 D Daug Bm Daug D Daug Bm D
hun - ky, ton - key way. "Ab - a, dab - a, dab - a, dab - a, dab - a, dab - a dab," means
TAB

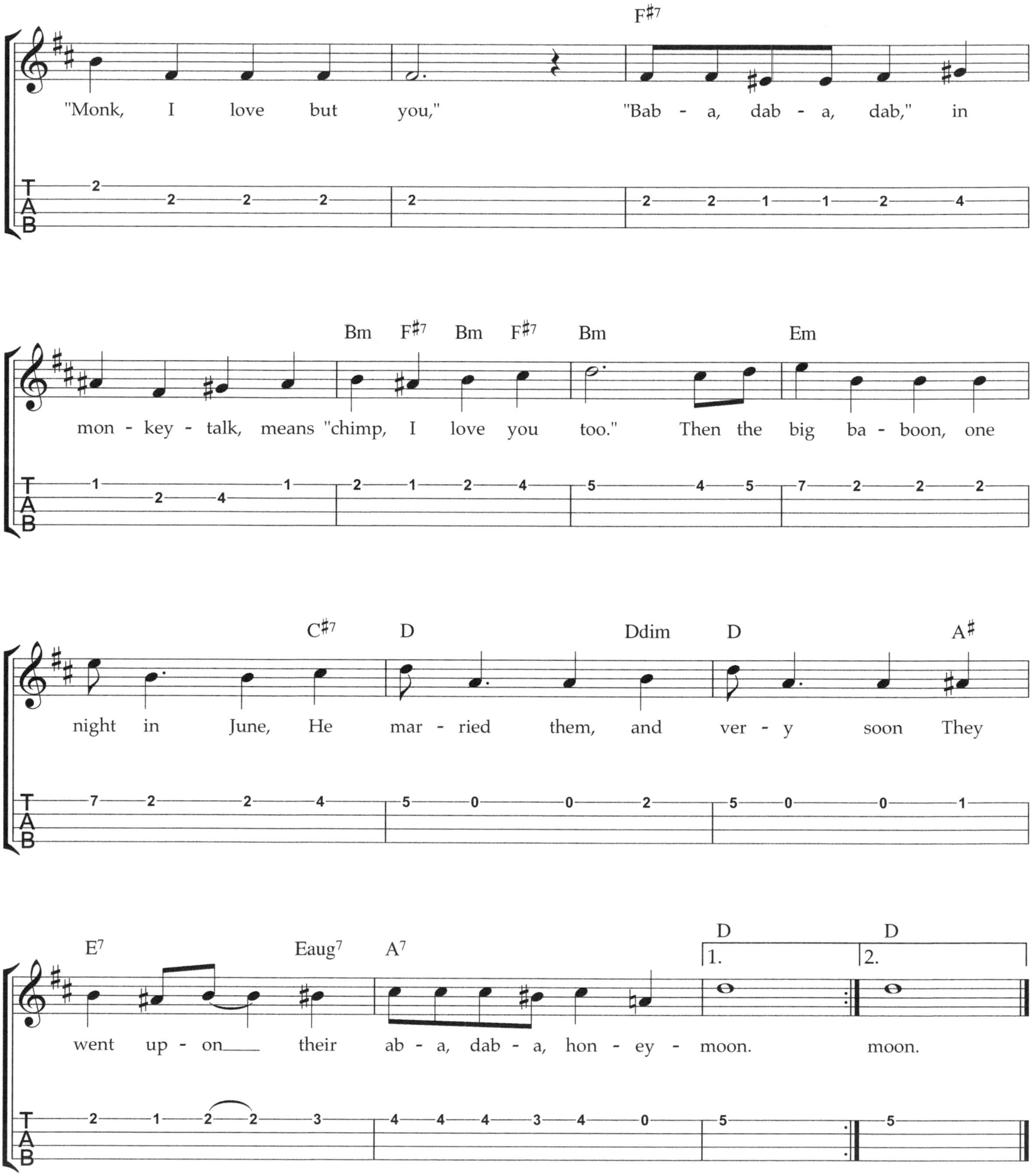
F#7
"Monk, I love but you," "Bab - a, dab - a, dab," in
Bm F#7 Bm F#7 Bm Em
mon - key - talk, means "chimp, I love you too." Then the big ba - boon, one
C#7 D Ddim D A#
night in June, He mar - ried them, and ver - y soon They
E7 Eaug7 A7 D D
went up - on their ab - a, dab - a, hon - ey - moon. moon.
1.
2.
TAB

After The Ball

by Charles K. Harris

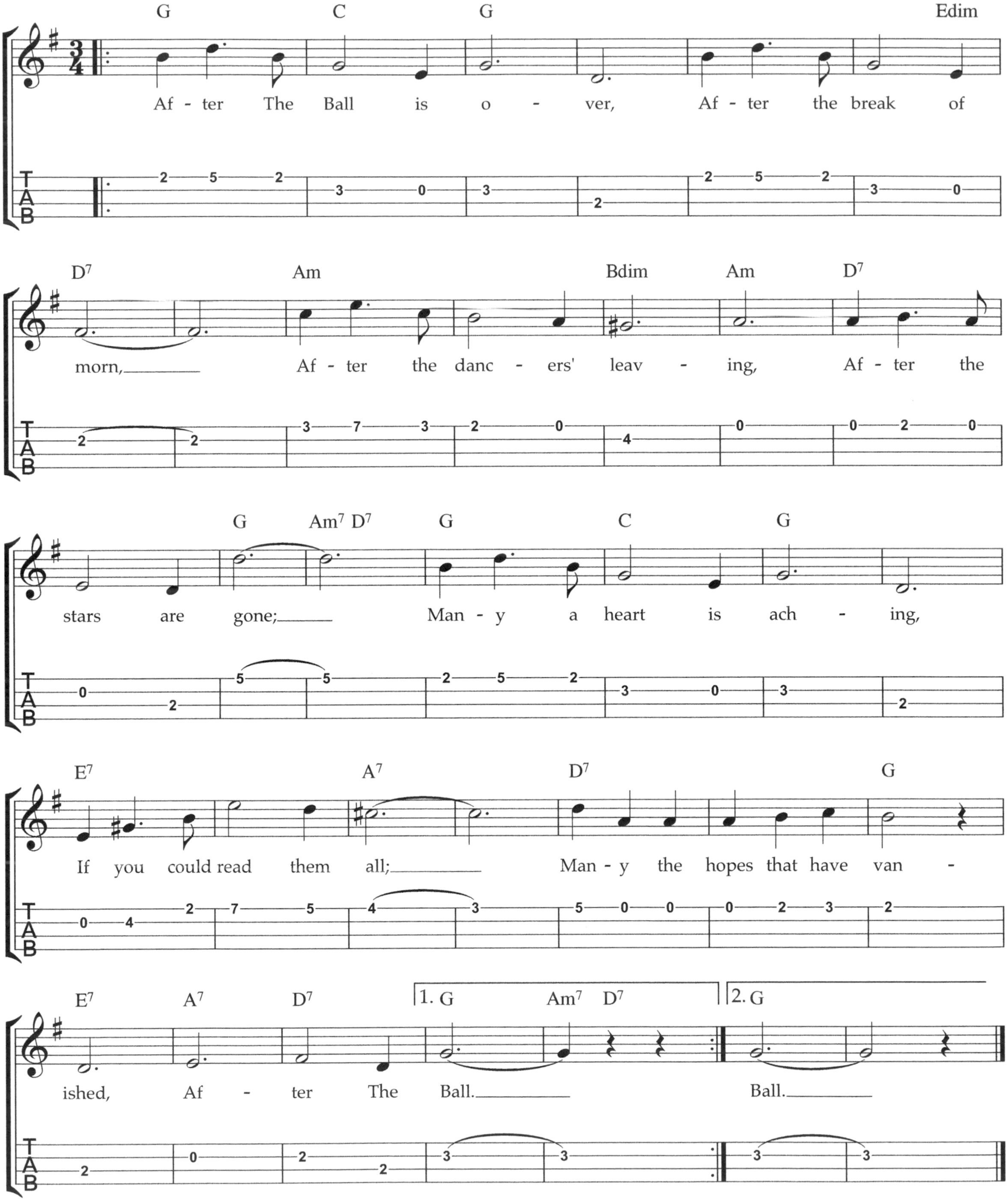
G C G Edim
Af - ter The Ball is o - ver, Af - ter the break of
D7 Am Bdim Am D7
morn, Af - ter the danc - ers' leav - ing, Af - ter the
G Am7 D7 G C G
stars are gone; Man - y a heart is ach - ing,
E7 A7 D7 G
If you could read them all; Man - y the hopes that have van -
E7 A7 D7 1. G Am7 D7 2. G
ished, Af - ter The Ball. Ball.
TAB

Akahi Hoi

H.M. King Kalakaua

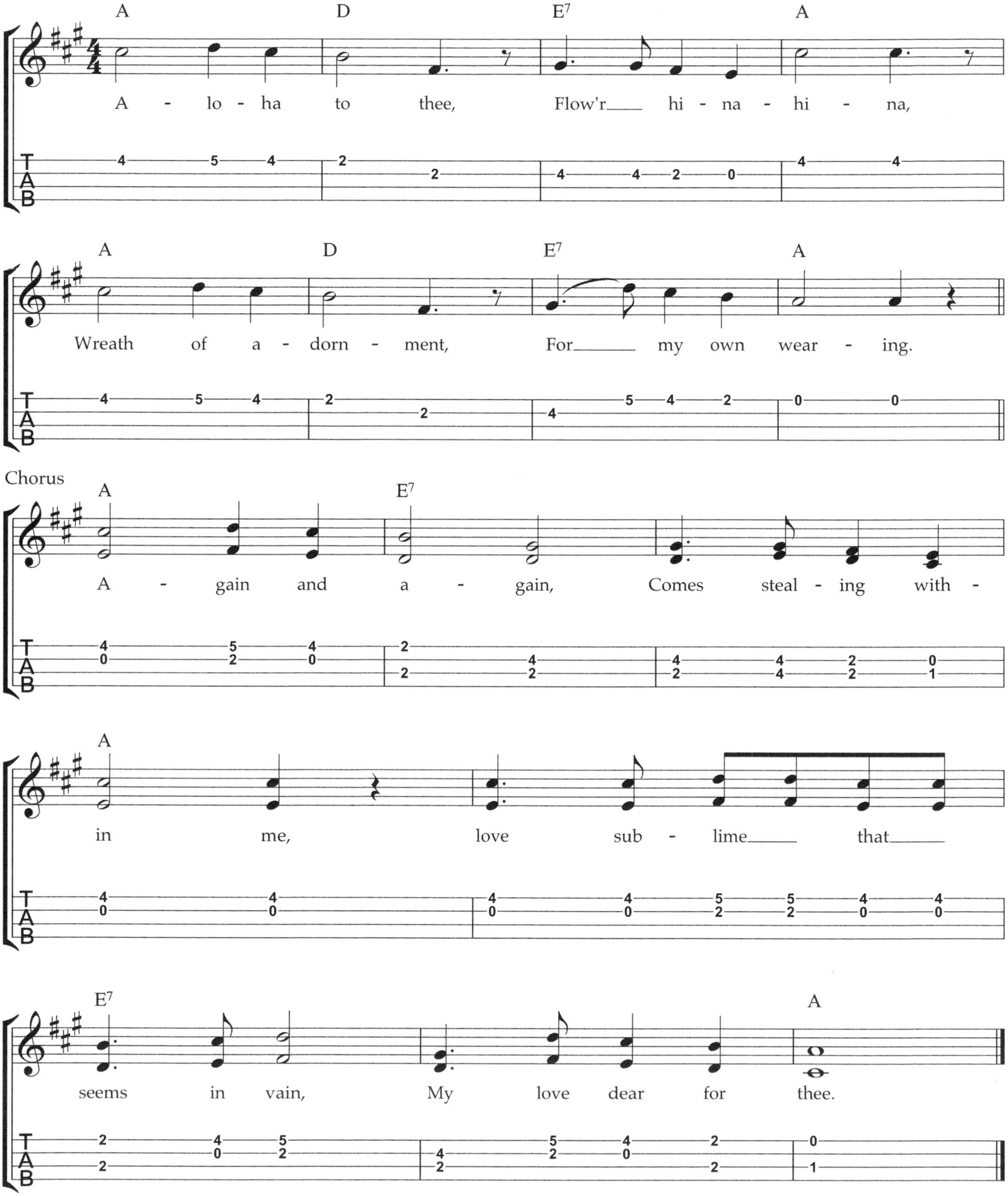
A D E7 A
A - lo - ha to thee, Flow'r hi - na - hi - na,
A D E7 A
Wreath of a - dorn - ment, For my own wear - ing.
Chorus
A E7
A - gain and a - gain, Comes steal - ing with -
A
in me, love sub - lime that
E7 A
seems in vain, My love dear for thee.

Aloha E Ka Pua

Chas. E. King
Burrows

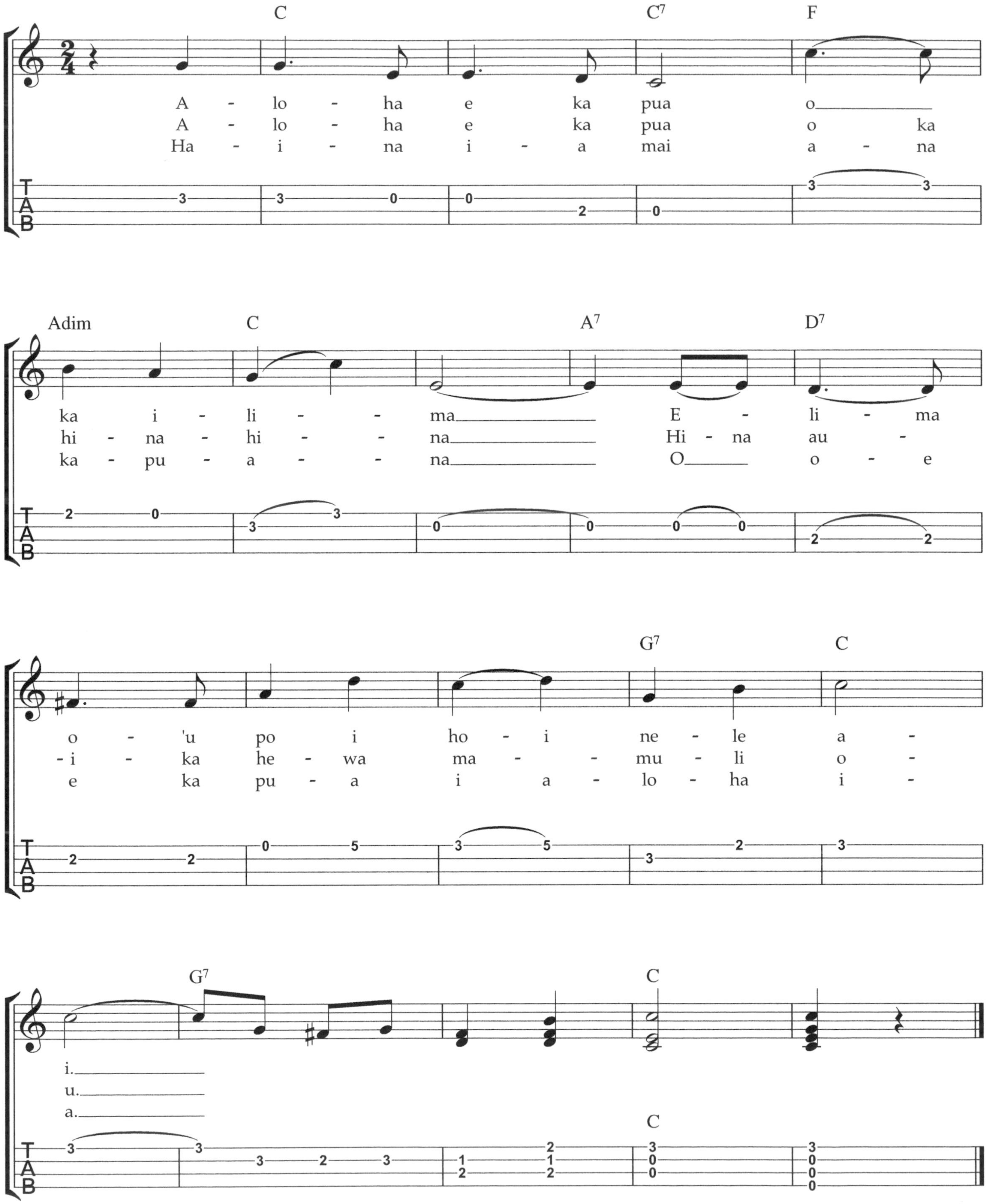
C C7 F
A - lo - ha e ka pua o
A - lo - ha e ka pua o ka
Ha - i - na i - a mai a - na
Adim C A7 D7
ka i - li - - ma E - li - ma
hi - na - hi - - na Hi - na au -
ka - pu - a - - na O o - e
G7 C
o - 'u po i ho - i ne - le a -
- i - ka he - wa ma - - mu - li o -
e ka pu - a i a - lo - ha i -
G7 C
i.
u.
a.
C

Angelina Baker

Music by
Stephen Foster

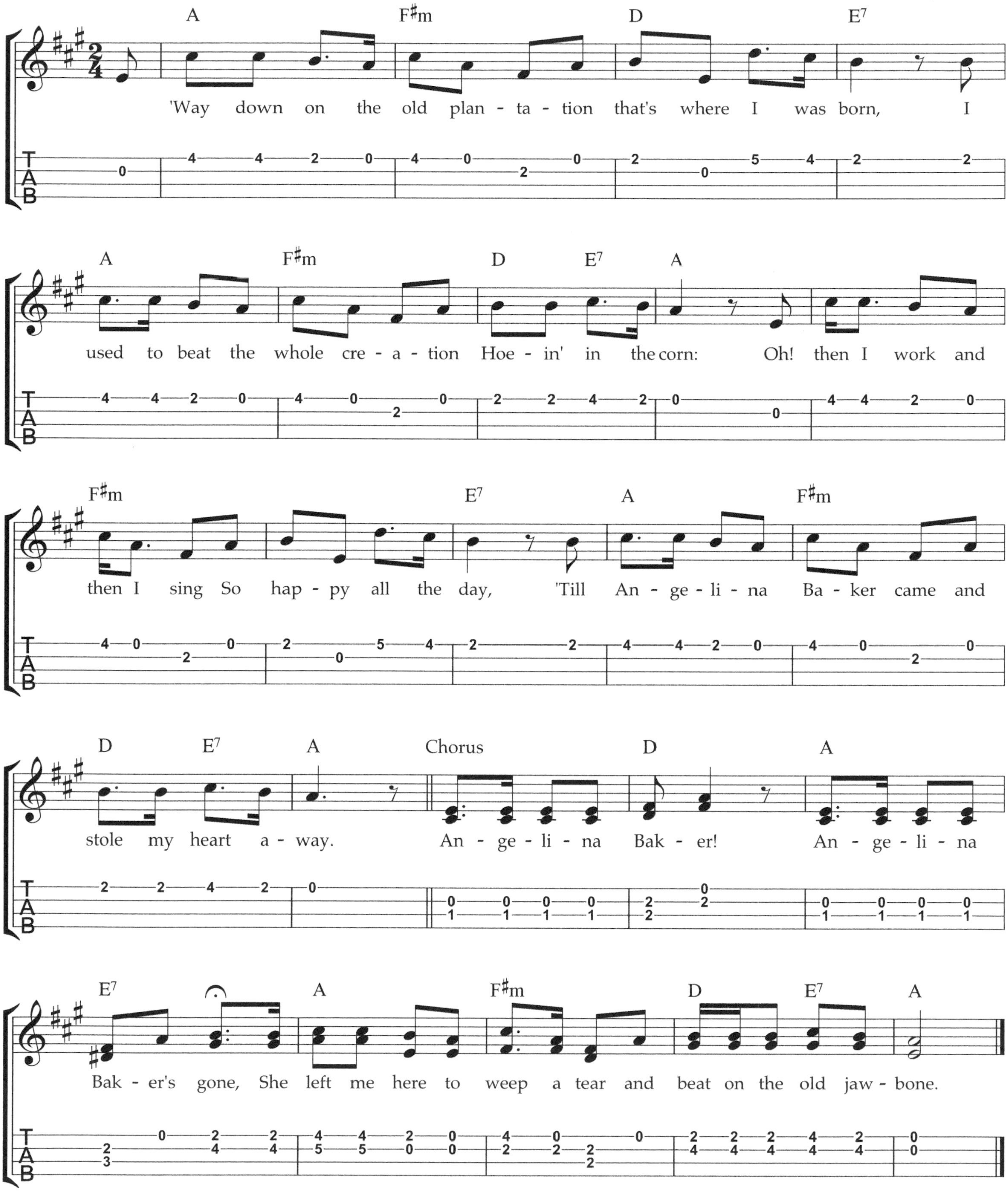
A F♯m D E7
'Way down on the old plan - ta - tion that's where I was born, I
A F♯m D E7 A
used to beat the whole cre - a - tion Hoe - in' in the corn: Oh! then I work and
F♯m E7 A F♯m
then I sing So hap - py all the day, 'Till An - ge - li - na Ba - ker came and
D E7 A Chorus D A
stole my heart a - way. An - ge - li - na Bak - er! An - ge - li - na
E7 A F♯m D E7 A
Bak - er's gone, She left me here to weep a tear and beat on the old jaw - bone.
TAB

China Boy

Words and Music by
Dick Winfree and Phil Boutelje

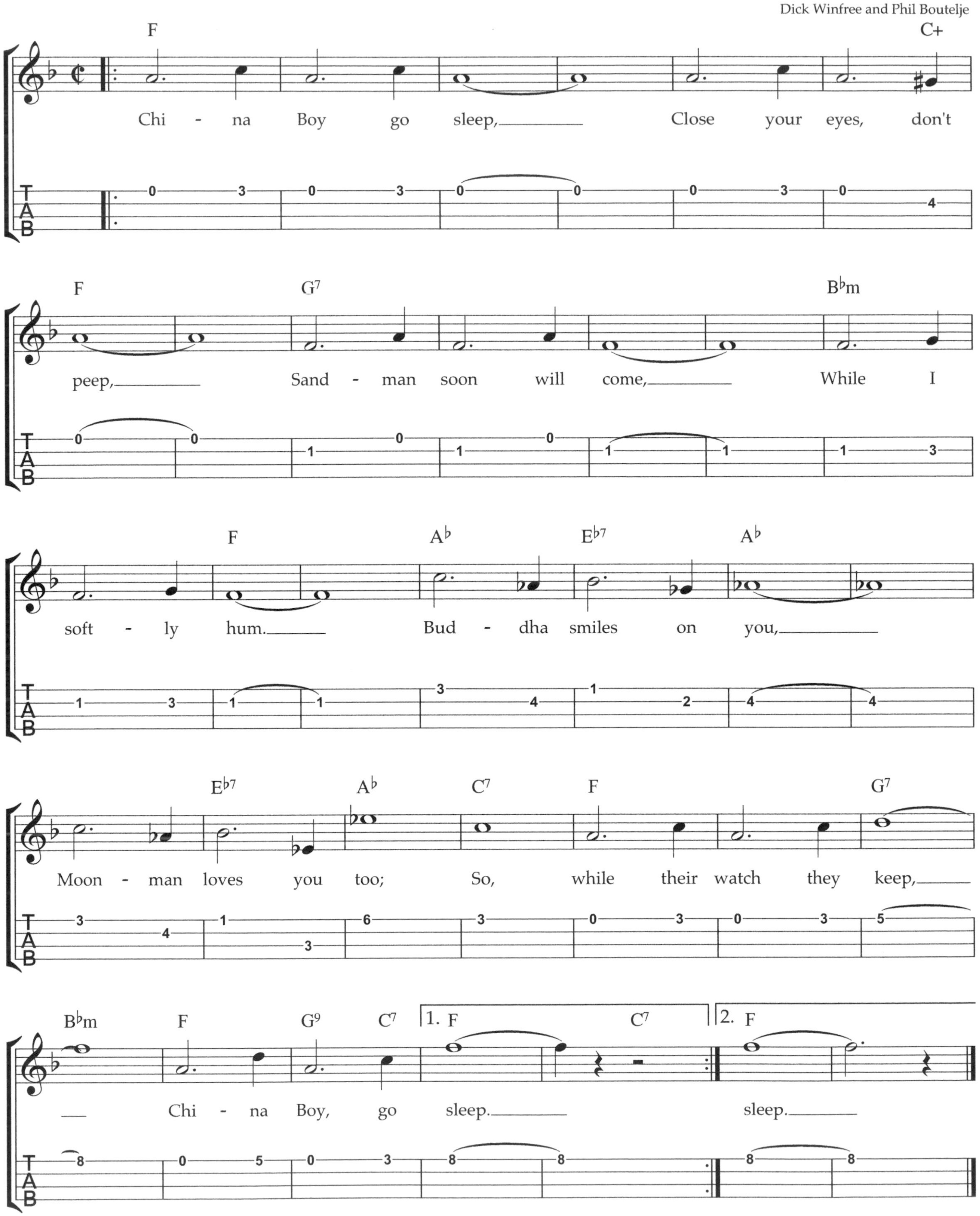
F C+
Chi - na Boy go sleep, Close your eyes, don't
F G7 B♭m
peep, Sand - man soon will come, While I
F A♭ E♭7 A♭
soft - ly hum. Bud - dha smiles on you,
E♭7 A♭ C7 F G7
Moon - man loves you too; So, while their watch they keep,
B♭m F G9 C7 1. F C7 2. F
Chi - na Boy, go sleep. sleep.
TAB

The Colorado Trail

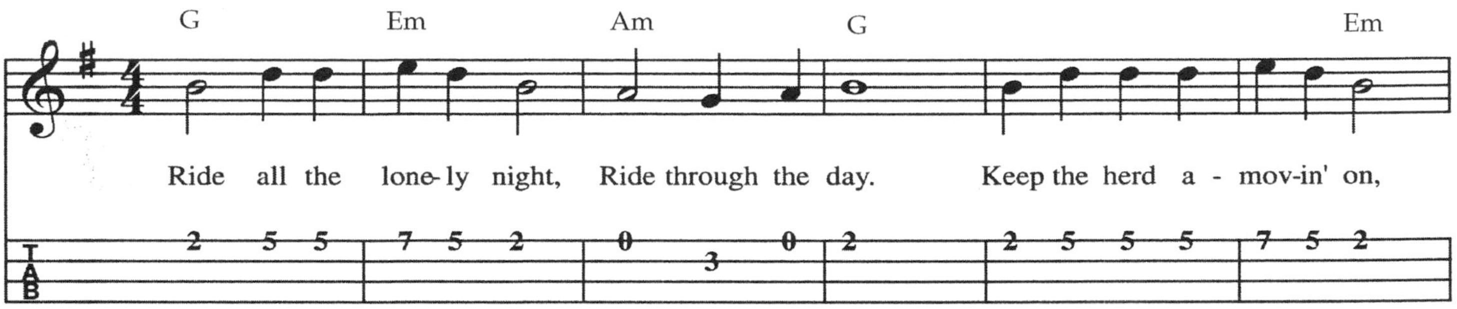

G Em Am G Em
Ride all the lone-ly night, Ride through the day. Keep the herd a - mov-in' on,

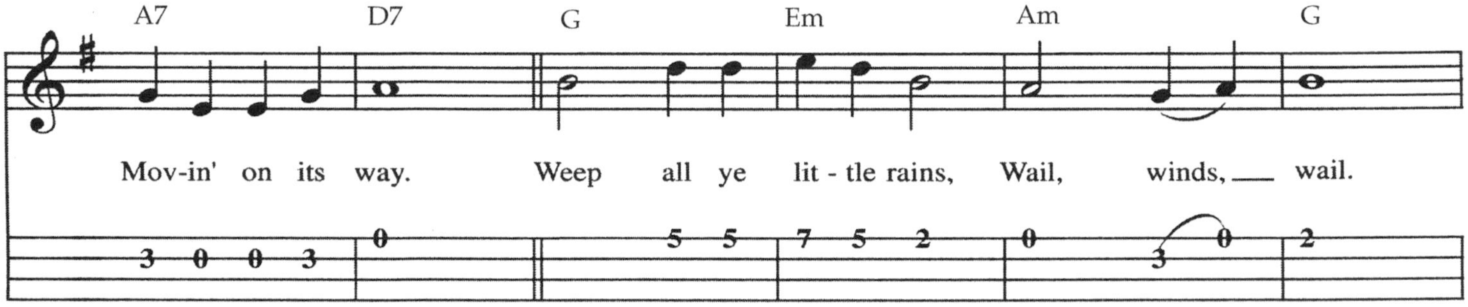

A7 D7 G Em Am G
Mov-in' on its way. Weep all ye lit - tle rains, Wail, winds, wail.

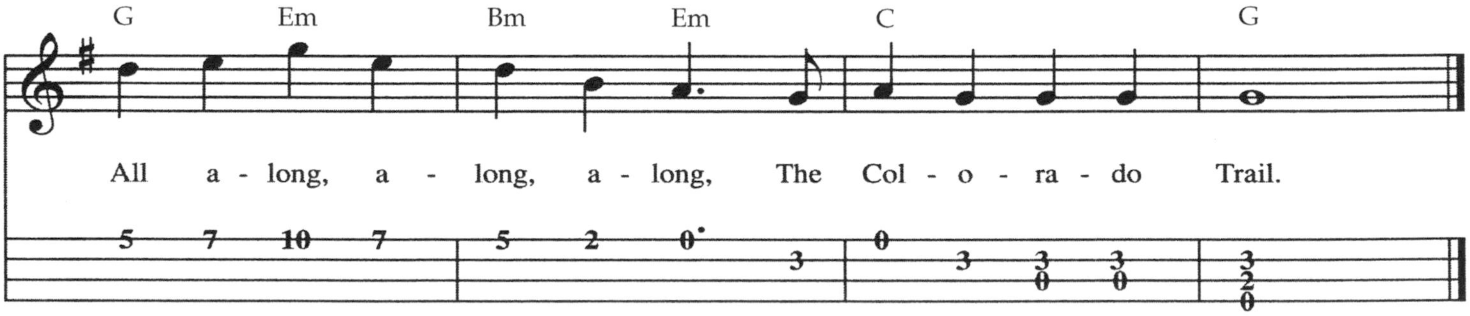

G Em Bm Em C G
All a - long, a - long, a - long, The Col - o - ra - do Trail.

The Darktown Strutters' Ball

Words and music by
Shelton Brooks

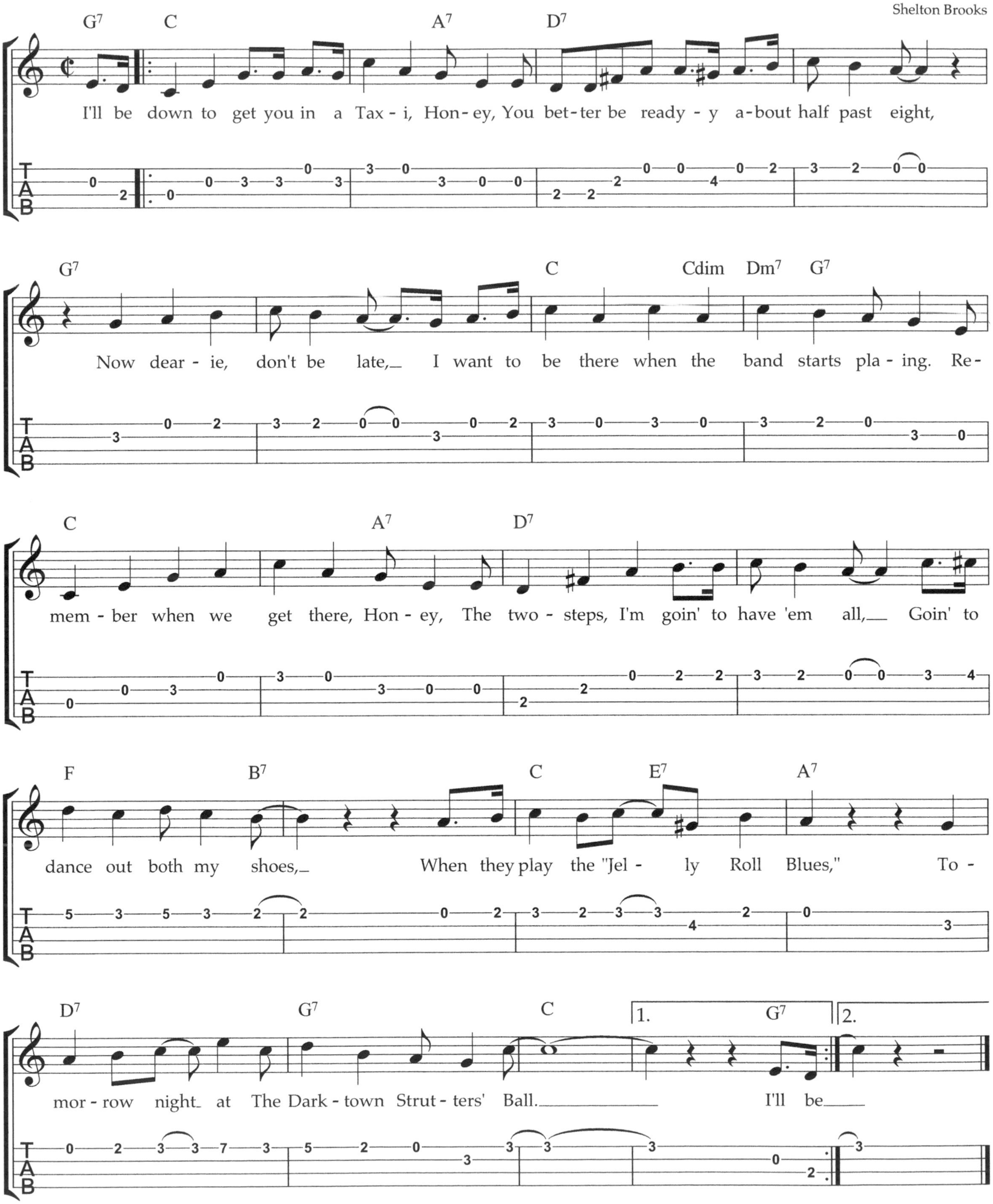
G7 C A7 D7
I'll be down to get you in a Tax - i, Hon - ey, You bet - ter be ready - y a - bout half past eight,
G7 C Cdim Dm7 G7
Now dear - ie, don't be late,_ I want to be there when the band starts pla - ing. Re -
C A7 D7
mem - ber when we get there, Hon - ey, The two - steps, I'm goin' to have 'em all,_ Goin' to
F B7 C E7 A7
dance out both my shoes,_ When they play the "Jel - ly Roll Blues," To -
D7 G7 C 1. G7 2.
mor - row night_ at The Dark - town Strut - ters' Ball._ I'll be_

Five Foot Two, Eyes Of Blue

Lyrics by
Sam Lewis and
Joe Young

Music by
Ray Henderson

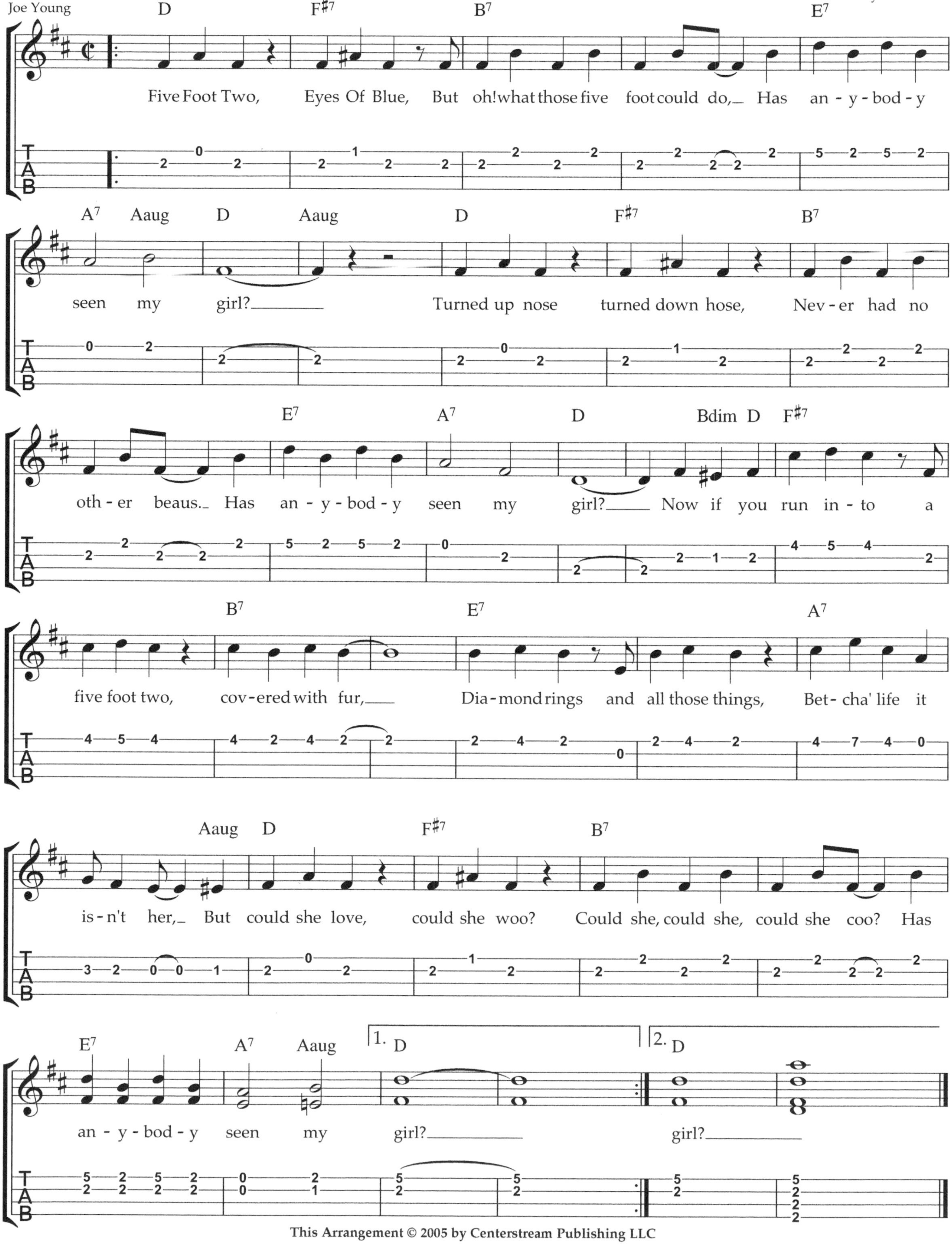
D F#7 B7 E7
Five Foot Two, Eyes Of Blue, But oh! what those five foot could do, Has an-y-bod-y
A7 Aaug D Aaug D F#7 B7
seen my girl? Turned up nose turned down hose, Nev-er had no
E7 A7 D Bdim D F#7
oth-er beaus. Has an-y-bod-y seen my girl? Now if you run in-to a
B7 E7 A7
five foot two, cov-ered with fur, Dia-mond rings and all those things, Bet-cha' life it
Aaug D F#7 B7
is-n't her, But could she love, could she woo? Could she, could she, could she coo? Has
E7 A7 Aaug 1. D 2. D
an-y-bod-y seen my girl? girl?

Gentle Annie

Music by
Stephen Foster

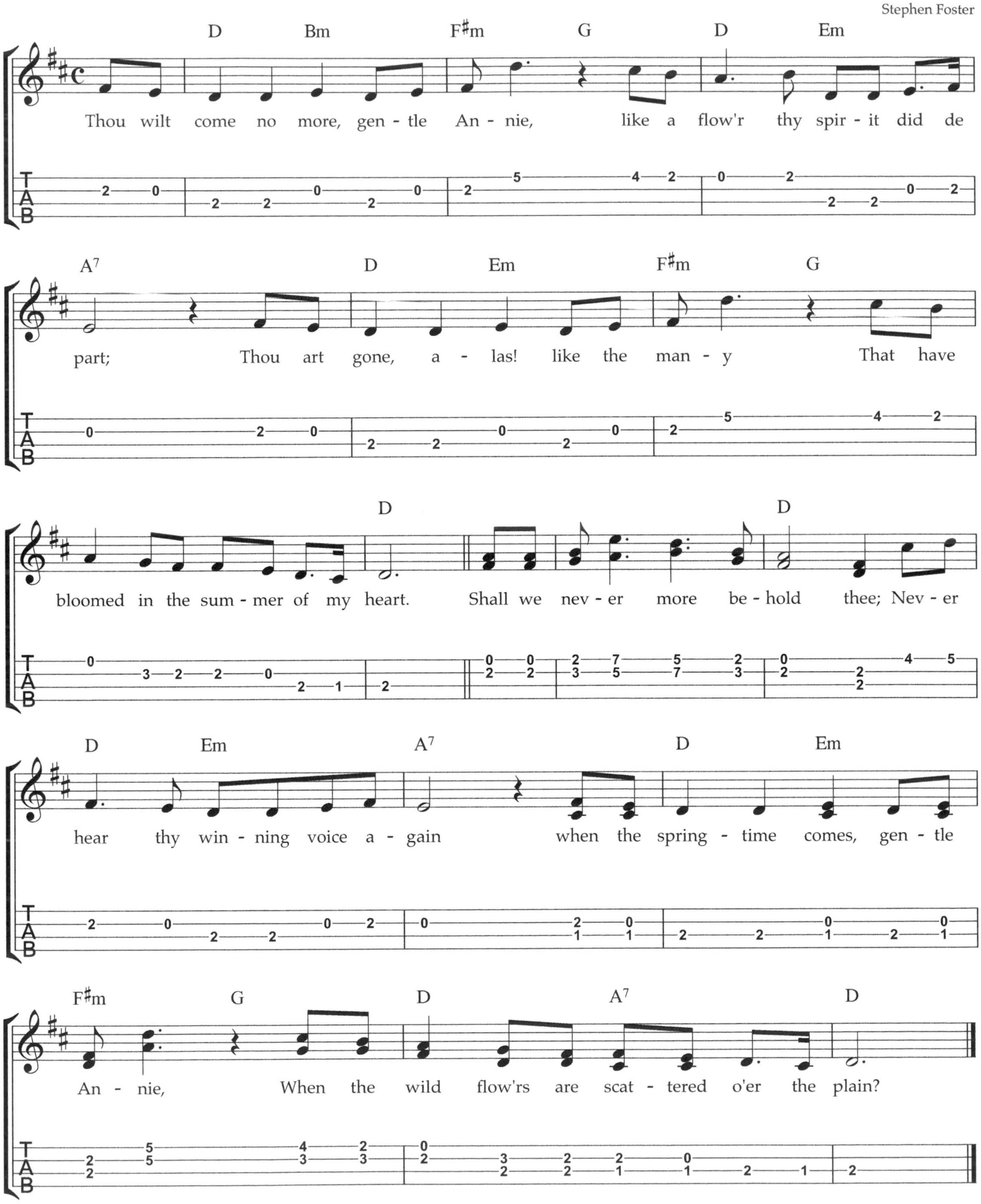
D Bm F♯m G D Em
Thou wilt come no more, gen - tle An - nie, like a flow'r thy spir - it did de
A7 D Em F♯m G
part; Thou art gone, a - las! like the man - y That have
D D
bloomed in the sum - mer of my heart. Shall we nev - er more be - hold thee; Nev - er
D Em A7 D Em
hear thy win - ning voice a - gain when the spring - time comes, gen - tle
F♯m G D A7 D
An - nie, When the wild flow'rs are scat - tered o'er the plain?

Git Along Little Dogies

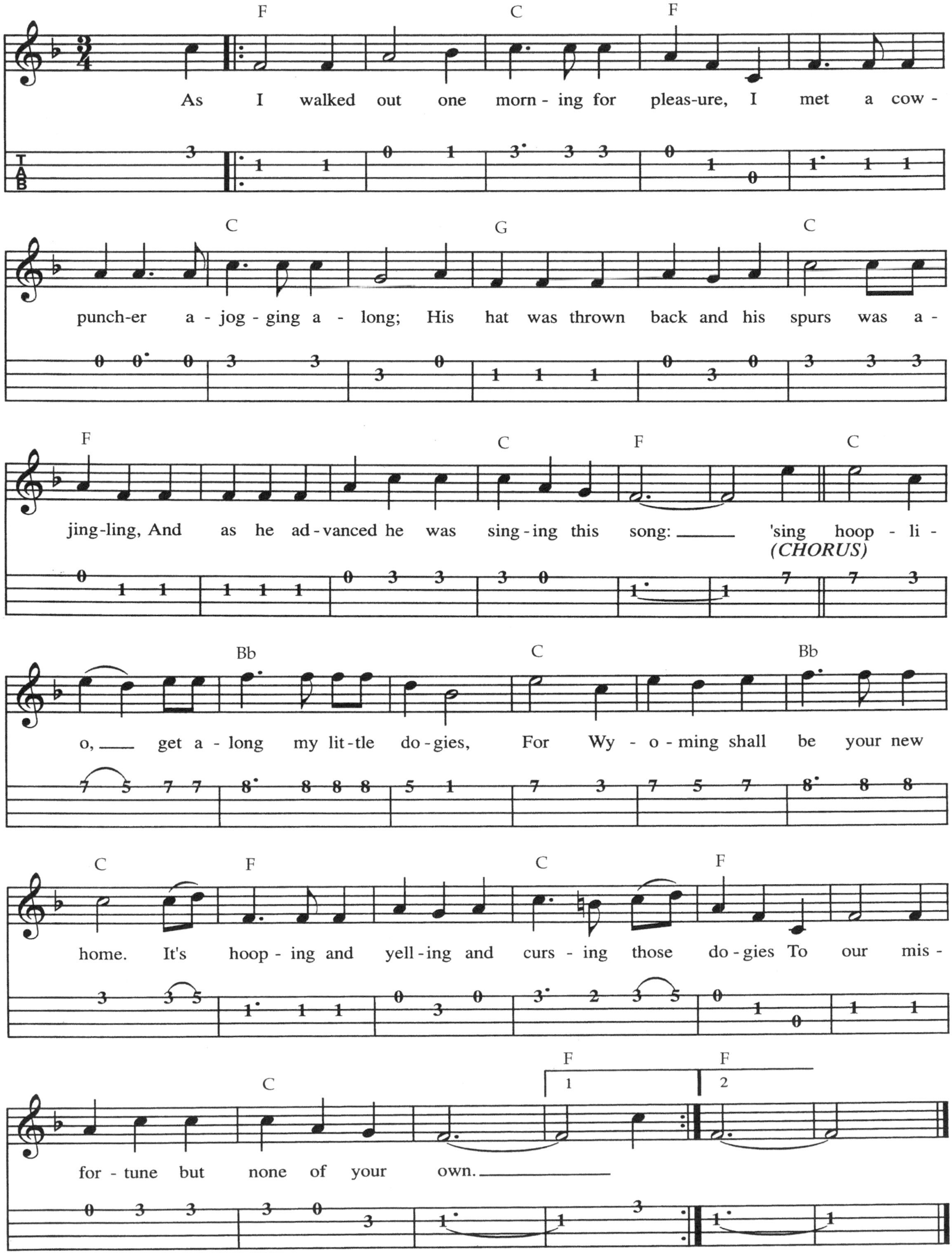

As I walked out one morn - ing for pleas-ure, I met a cow -
punch-er a - jog - ging a - long; His hat was thrown back and his spurs was a -
jing-ling, And as he ad - vanced he was sing - ing this song: 'sing hoop - li -
(CHORUS)
o, get a - long my lit-tle do-gies, For Wy - o - ming shall be your new
home. It's hoop - ing and yell - ing and curs - ing those do - gies To our mis -
for - tune but none of your own.

The Glendy Burk

Music by
Stephen Foster

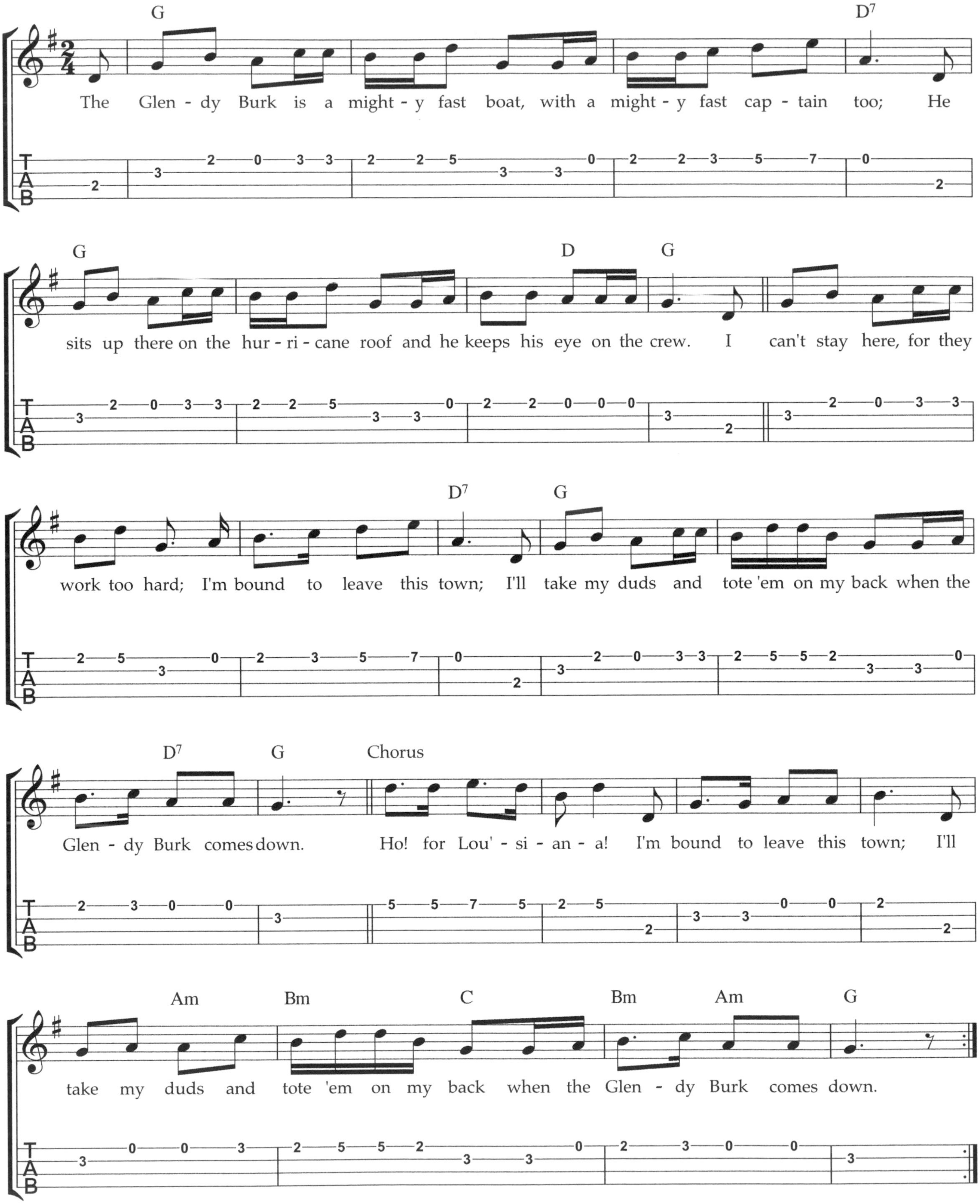
G
D7
The Glen - dy Burk is a might - y fast boat, with a might - y fast cap - tain too; He
G
D
G
sits up there on the hur - ri - cane roof and he keeps his eye on the crew. I can't stay here, for they
D7
G
work too hard; I'm bound to leave this town; I'll take my duds and tote 'em on my back when the
D7
G
Chorus
Glen - dy Burk comes down. Ho! for Lou' - si - an - a! I'm bound to leave this town; I'll
Am
Bm
C
Bm
Am
G
take my duds and tote 'em on my back when the Glen - dy Burk comes down.

Hard Times Come Again No More

Music by
Stephen Foster

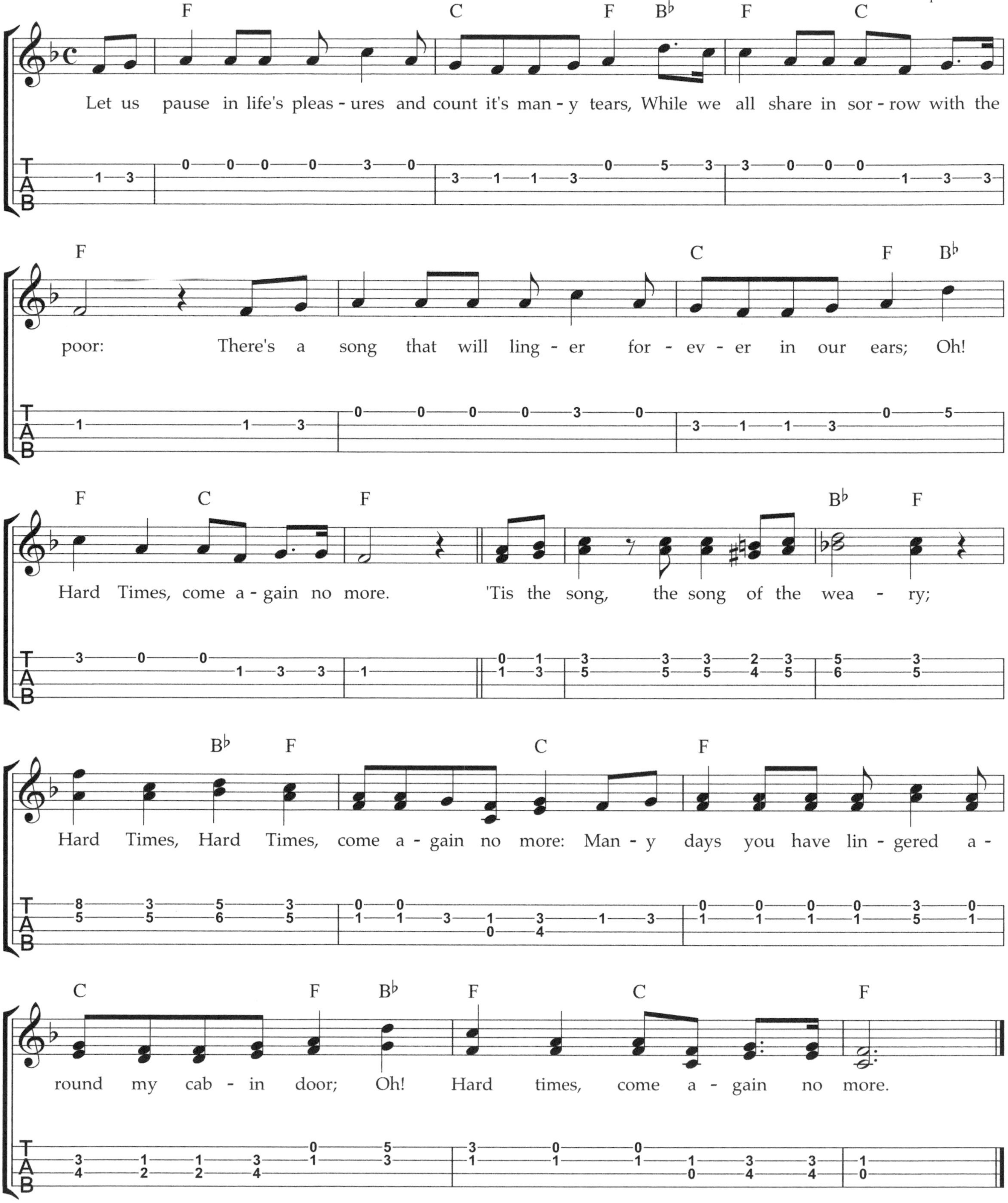
Let us pause in life's pleas - ures and count it's man - y tears, While we all share in sor - row with the
poor: There's a song that will ling - er for - ev - er in our ears; Oh!
Hard Times, come a - gain no more. 'Tis the song, the song of the wea - ry;
Hard Times, Hard Times, come a - gain no more: Man - y days you have lin - gered a -
round my cab - in door; Oh! Hard times, come a - gain no more.

Hawaii Ponoi

Words by King Kalalaua
Music by Prof. H.Berger

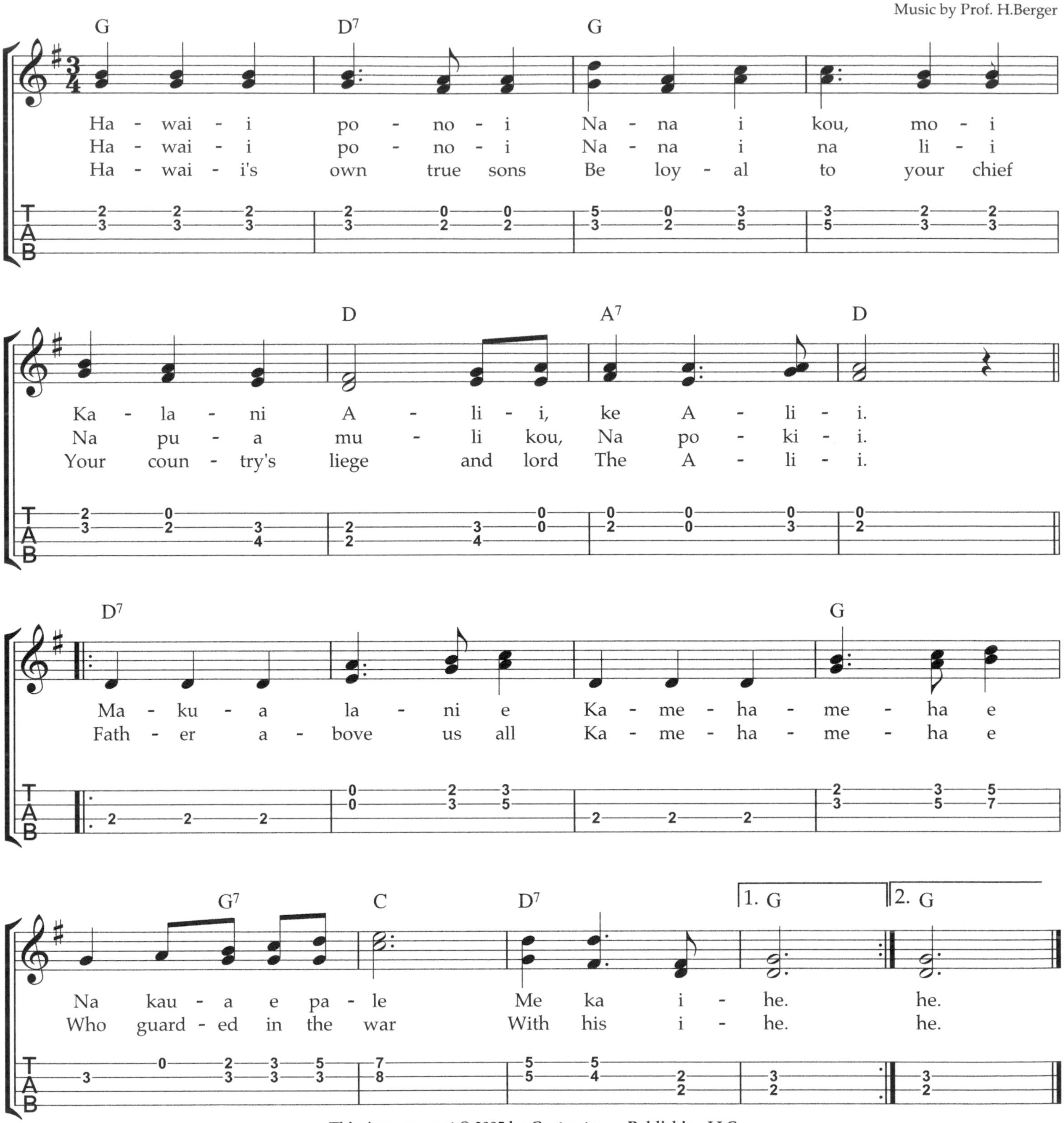
G D7 G
Ha - wai - i po - no - i Na - na i kou, mo - i
Ha - wai - i po - no - i Na - na i na li - i
Ha - wai - i's own true sons Be loy - al to your chief
D A7 D
Ka - la - ni A - li - i, ke A - li - i.
Na pu - a mu - li kou, Na po - ki - i.
Your coun - try's liege and lord The A - li - i.
D7 G
Ma - ku - a la - ni e Ka - me - ha - me - ha e
Fath - er a - bove us all Ka - me - ha - me - ha e
G7 C D7 1. G 2. G
Na kau - a e pa - le Me ka i - he. he.
Who guard - ed in the war With his i - he. he.

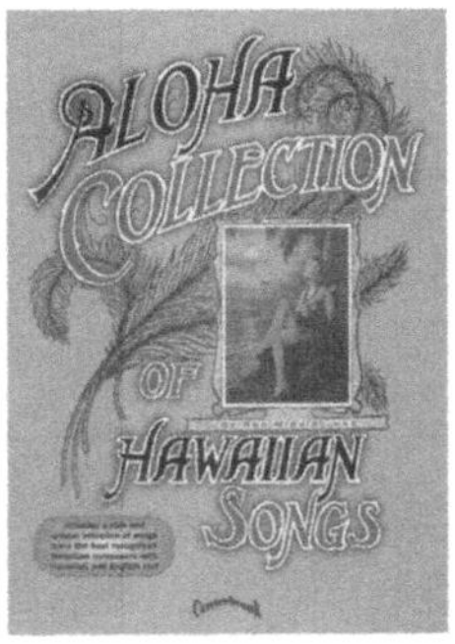
ALOHA
COLLECTION
OF
HAWAIIAN
SONGS

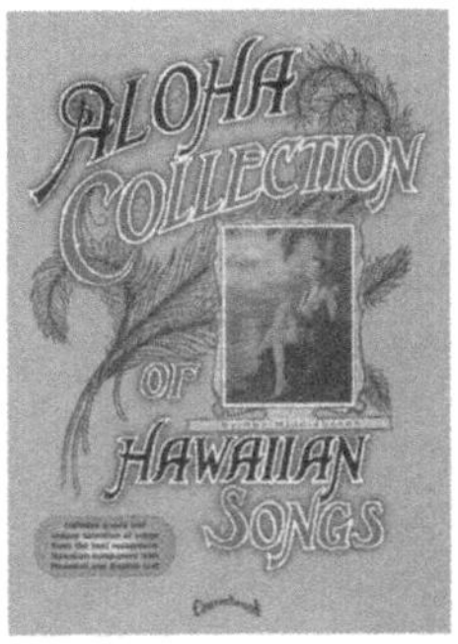
ALOHA
COLLECTION
OF
HAWAIIAN
SONGS

ALOHA
COLLECTION
OF
HAWAIIAN
SONGS

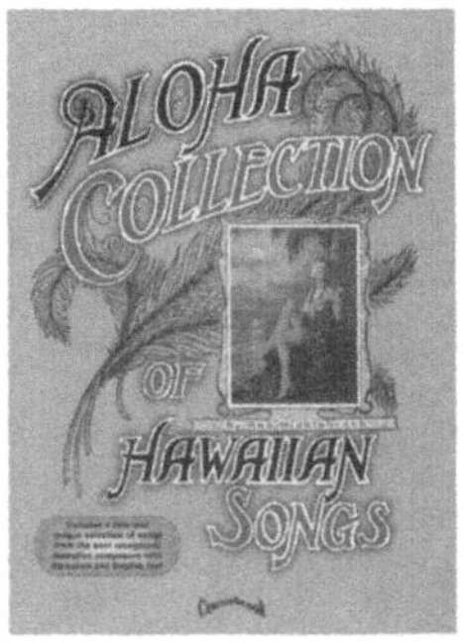
ALOHA
COLLECTION
OF
HAWAIIAN
SONGS

Honesakala

David Nape
Thomas Lindsey

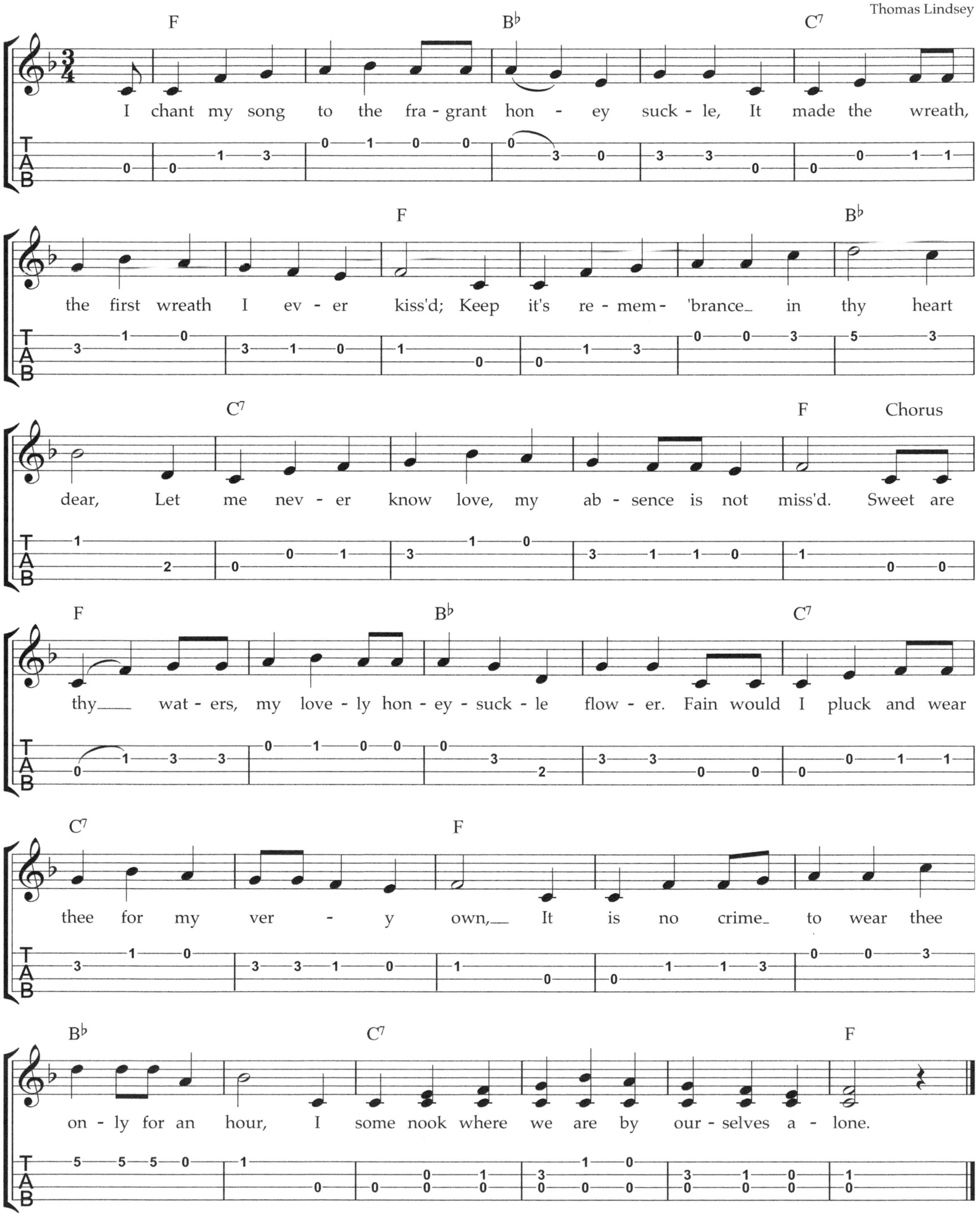
F Bb C7
I chant my song to the fra - grant hon - ey suck - le, It made the wreath,
T A B
F Bb
the first wreath I ev - er kiss'd; Keep it's re - mem - 'brance in thy heart
C7 F Chorus
dear, Let me nev - er know love, my ab - sence is not miss'd. Sweet are
F Bb C7
thy wat - ers, my love - ly hon - ey - suck - le flow - er. Fain would I pluck and wear
C7 F
thee for my ver - y own, It is no crime to wear thee
Bb C7 F
on - ly for an hour, I some nook where we are by our - selves a - lone.

Honolulu I Love You

Harry Lauder

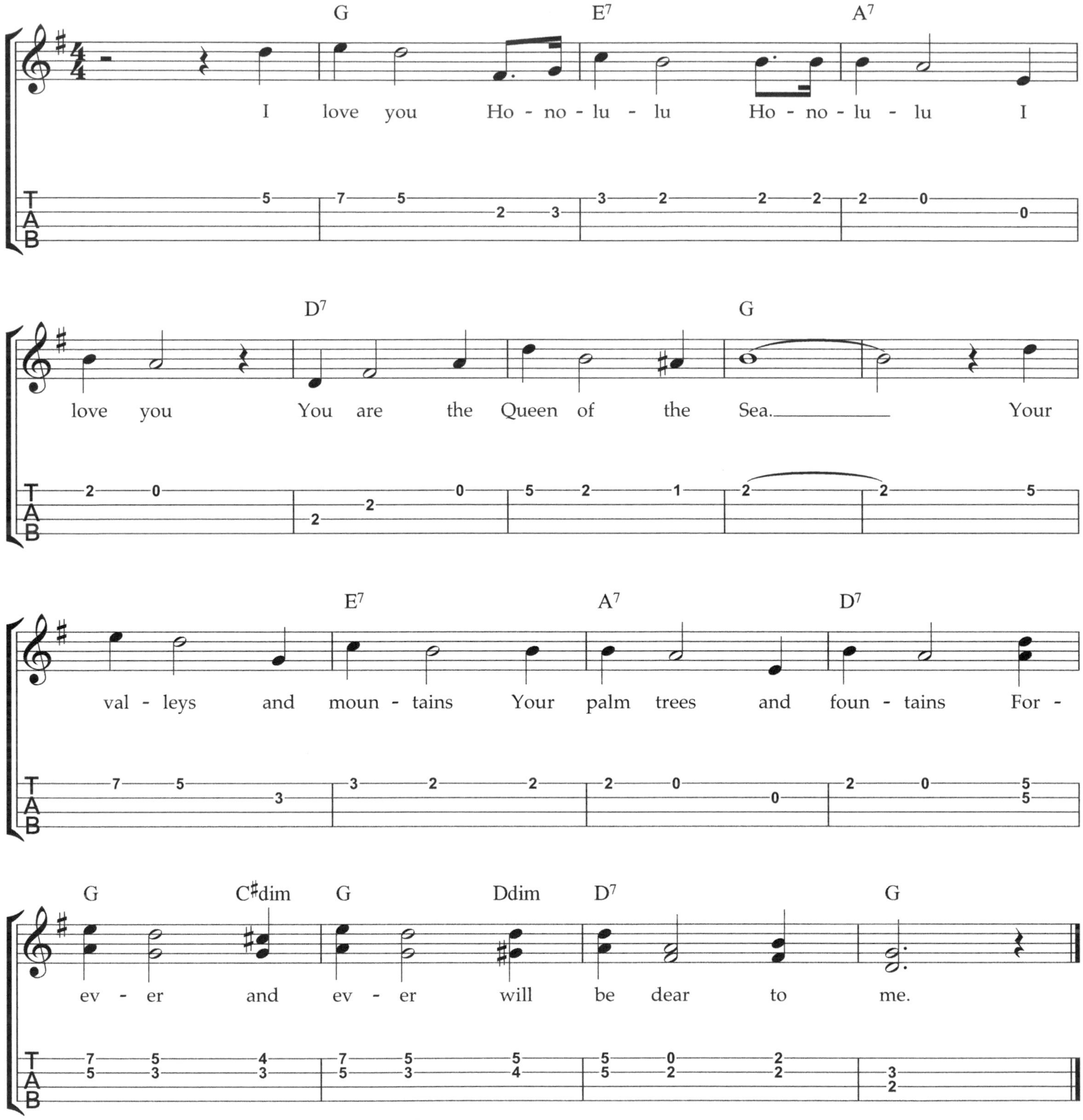
G E7 A7
I love you Ho - no - lu - lu Ho - no - lu - lu I
D7 G
love you You are the Queen of the Sea.
Your
E7 A7 D7
val - leys and moun - tains Your palm trees and foun - tains For -
G C#dim G Ddim D7 G
ev - er and ev - er will be dear to me.

HAWAIIAN UKULELE
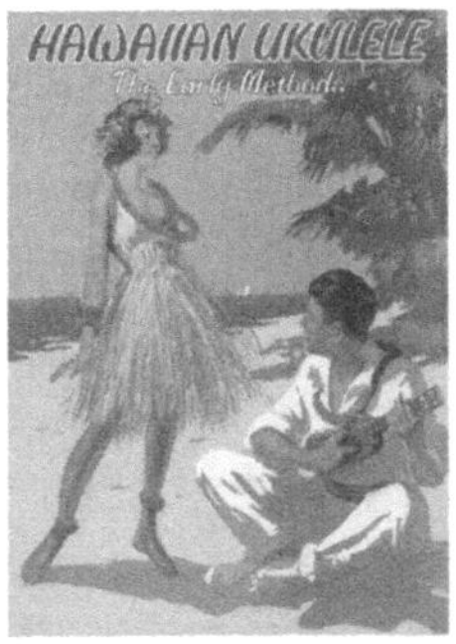
HAWAIIAN UKULELE

HAWAIIAN UKULELE
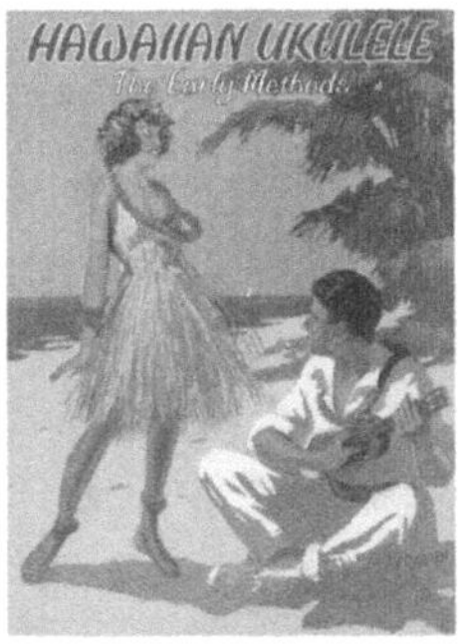
HAWAIIAN UKULELE

Hot Lips

by Henry Busse
Henry Lange and Lou Davis

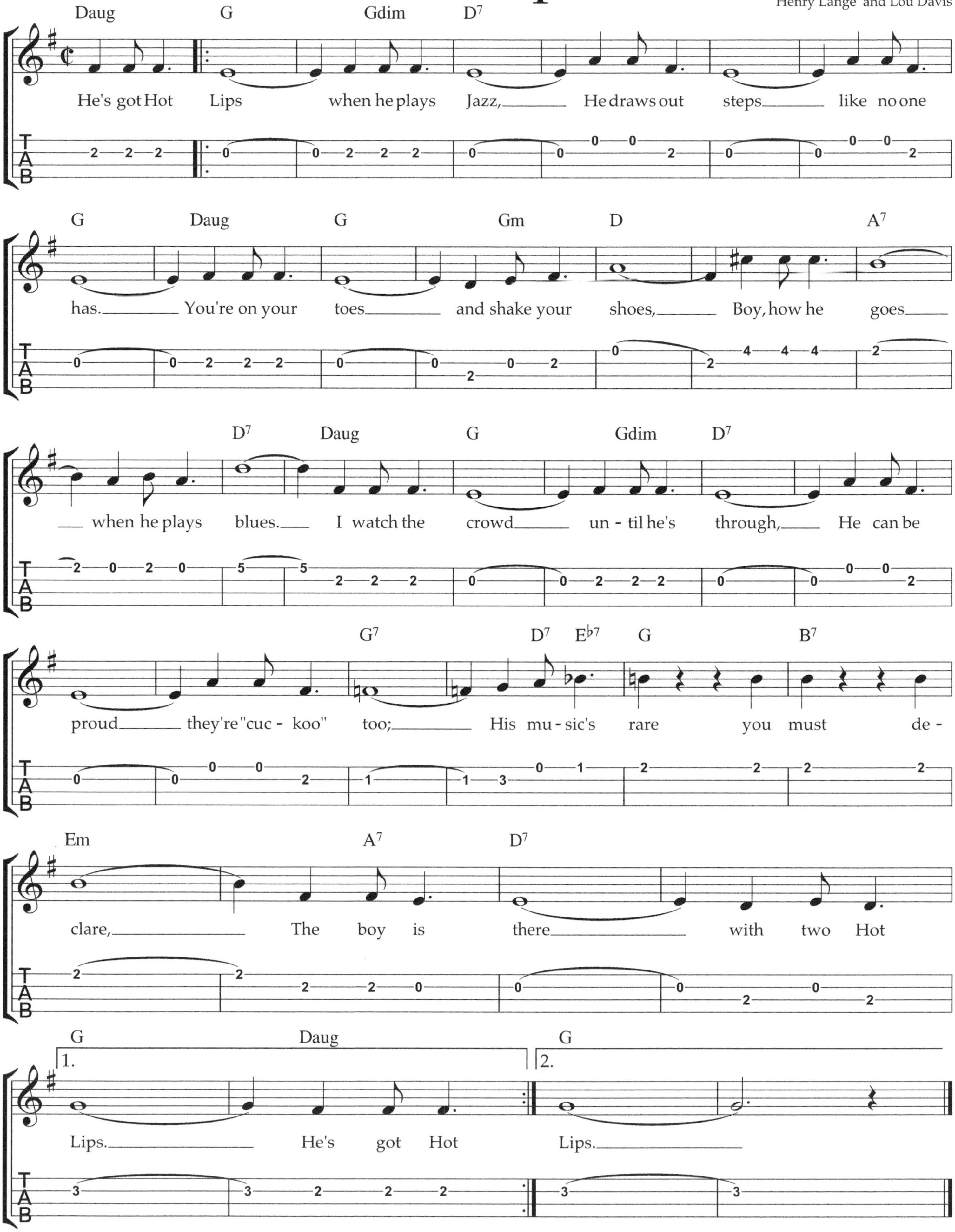
Daug G Gdim D7
He's got Hot Lips when he plays Jazz, He draws out steps like no one
G Daug G Gm D A7
has. You're on your toes and shake your shoes, Boy, how he goes
D7 Daug G Gdim D7
when he plays blues. I watch the crowd un - til he's through, He can be
G7 D7 E♭7 G B7
proud they're "cuc - koo" too; His mu - sic's rare you must de -
Em A7 D7
clare, The boy is there with two Hot
G Daug G
1. 2.
Lips. He's got Hot Lips.

I Cried for You

by Arthur Freed,
Gus Arnheim
and Abe Lyman

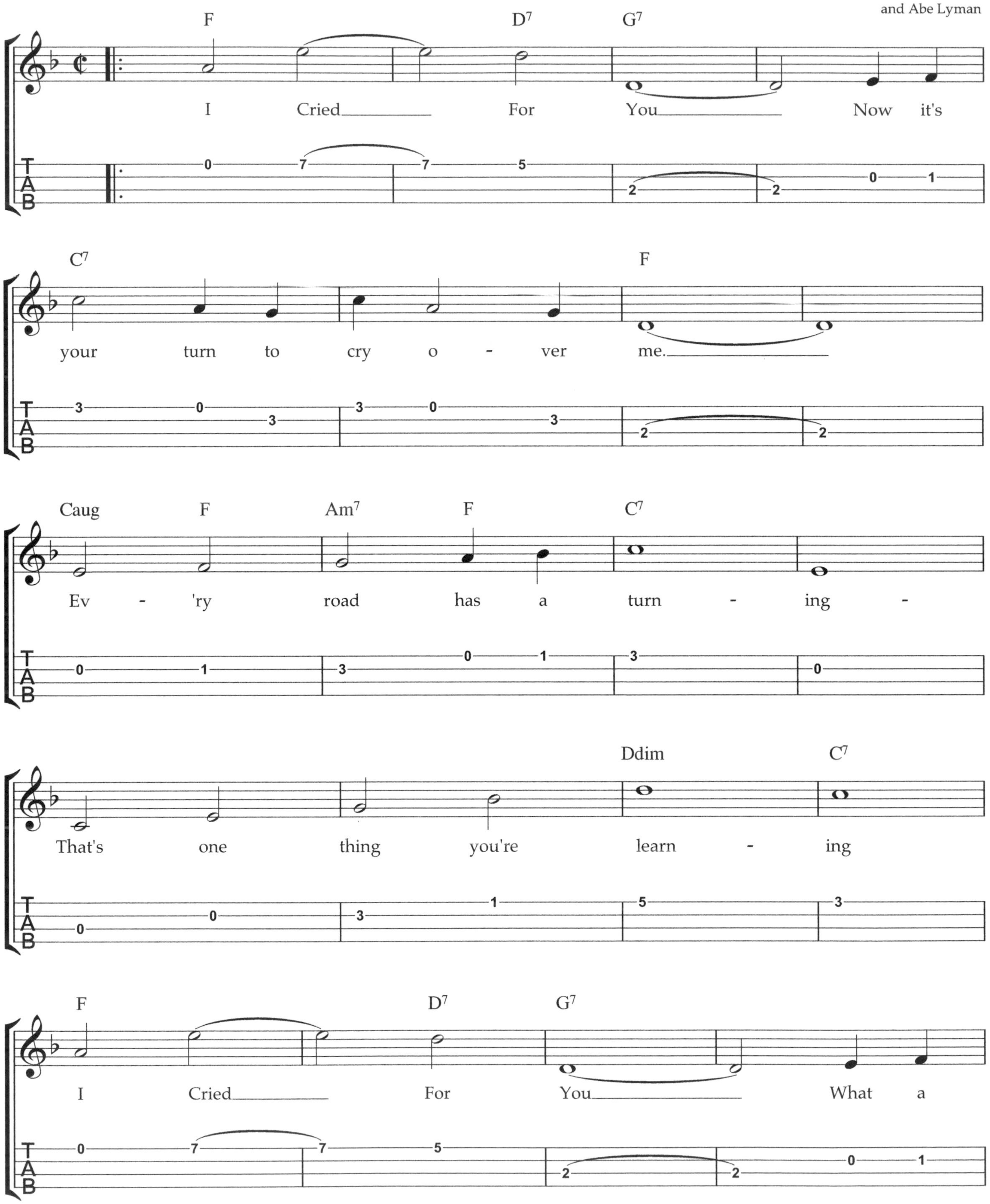
F D7 G7
I Cried For You Now it's
C7 F
your turn to cry o - ver me.
Caug F Am7 F C7
Ev - 'ry road has a turn - ing -
Ddim C7
That's one thing you're learn - ing
F D7 G7
I Cried For You What a

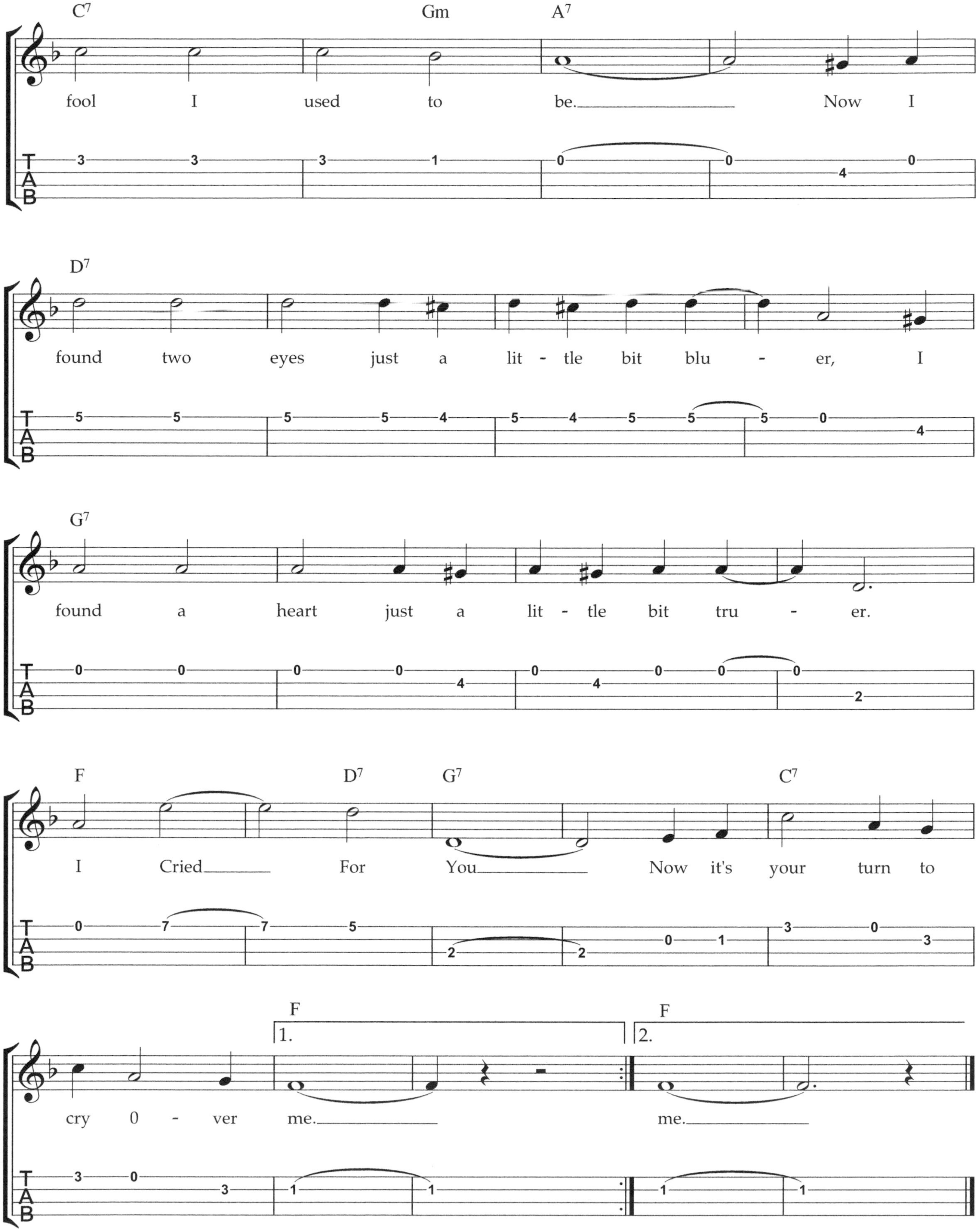
C7 Gm A7
fool I used to be. Now I
D7
found two eyes just a lit - tle bit blu - er, I
G7
found a heart just a lit - tle bit tru - er.
F D7 G7 C7
I Cried For You Now it's your turn to
F F
1. 2.
cry o - ver me. me.
T A B

I Love You

Lyrics by
Harlan Thompson

Music by
Harry Archer

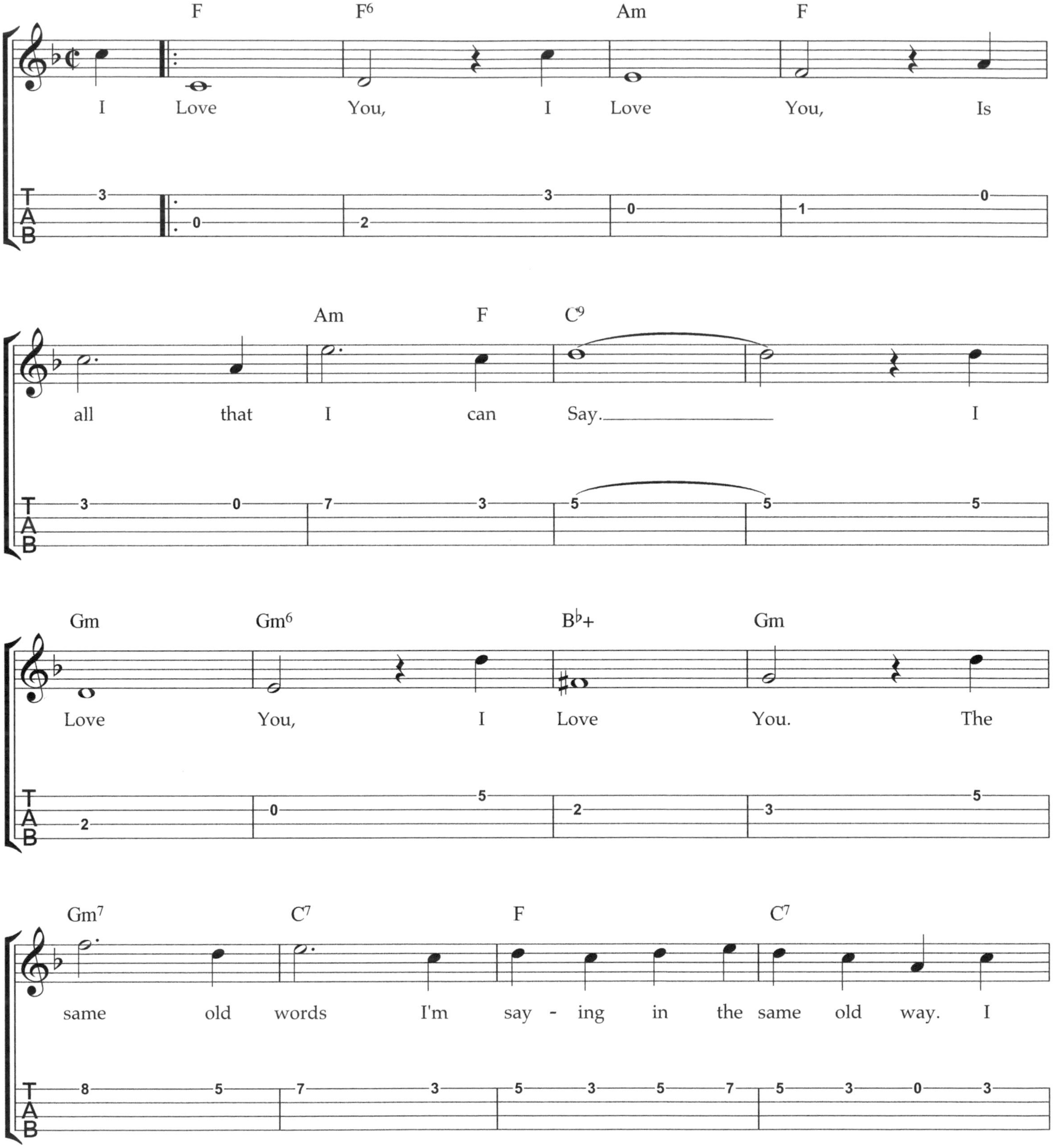
F F6 Am F
I Love You, I Love You, Is
Am F C9
all that I can Say. I
Gm Gm6 Bb+ Gm
Love You, I Love You. The
Gm7 C7 F C7
same old words I'm say - ing in the same old way. I

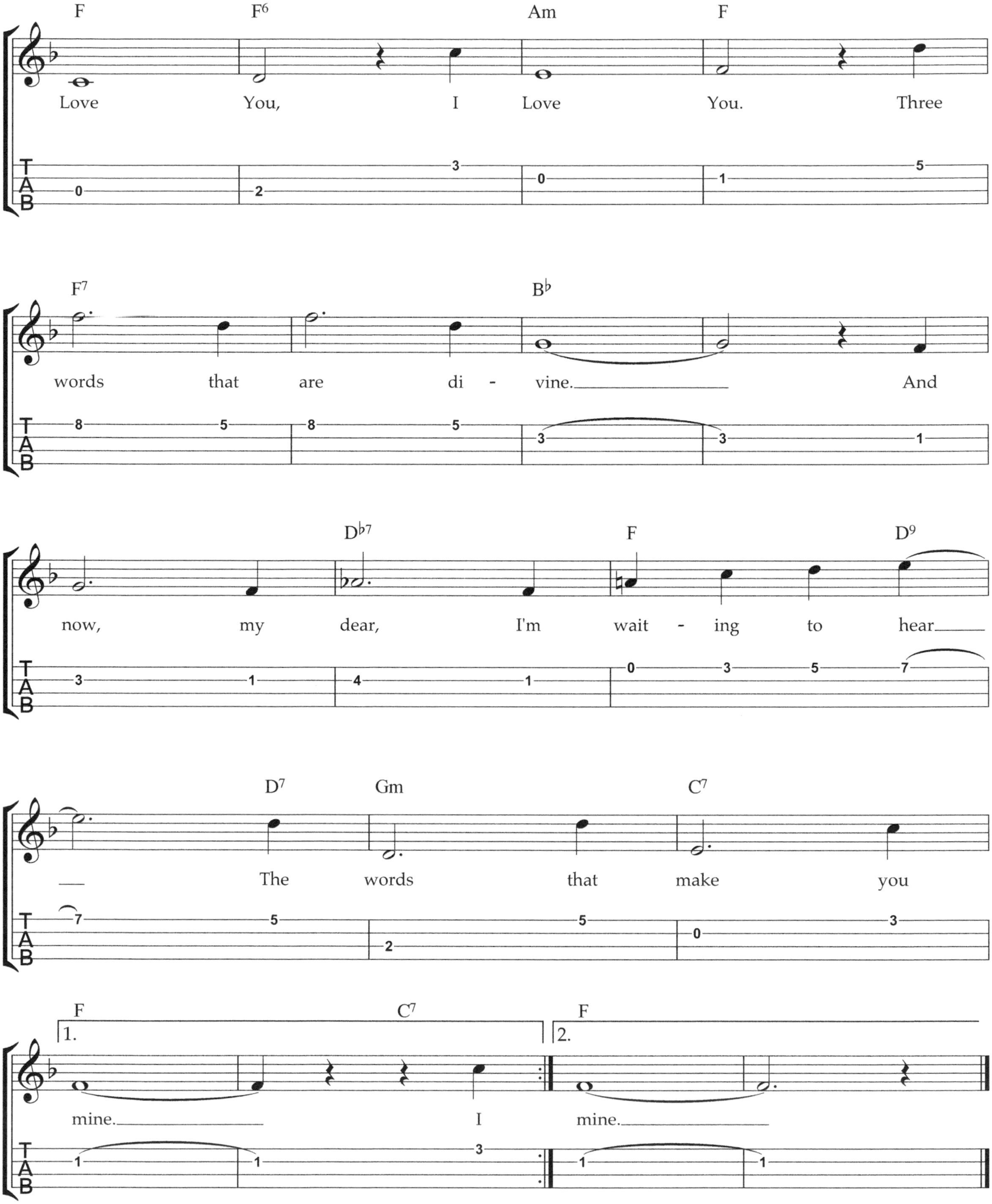
F F6 Am F
Love You, I Love You. Three
F7 B♭
words that are di - vine. And
D♭7 F D9
now, my dear, I'm wait - ing to hear
D7 Gm C7
The words that make you
F C7 F
1. 2.
mine. I mine.

I'm Always Chasing Rainbows

Lyric by
Joseph McCarthy

Music by
Harry Carroll

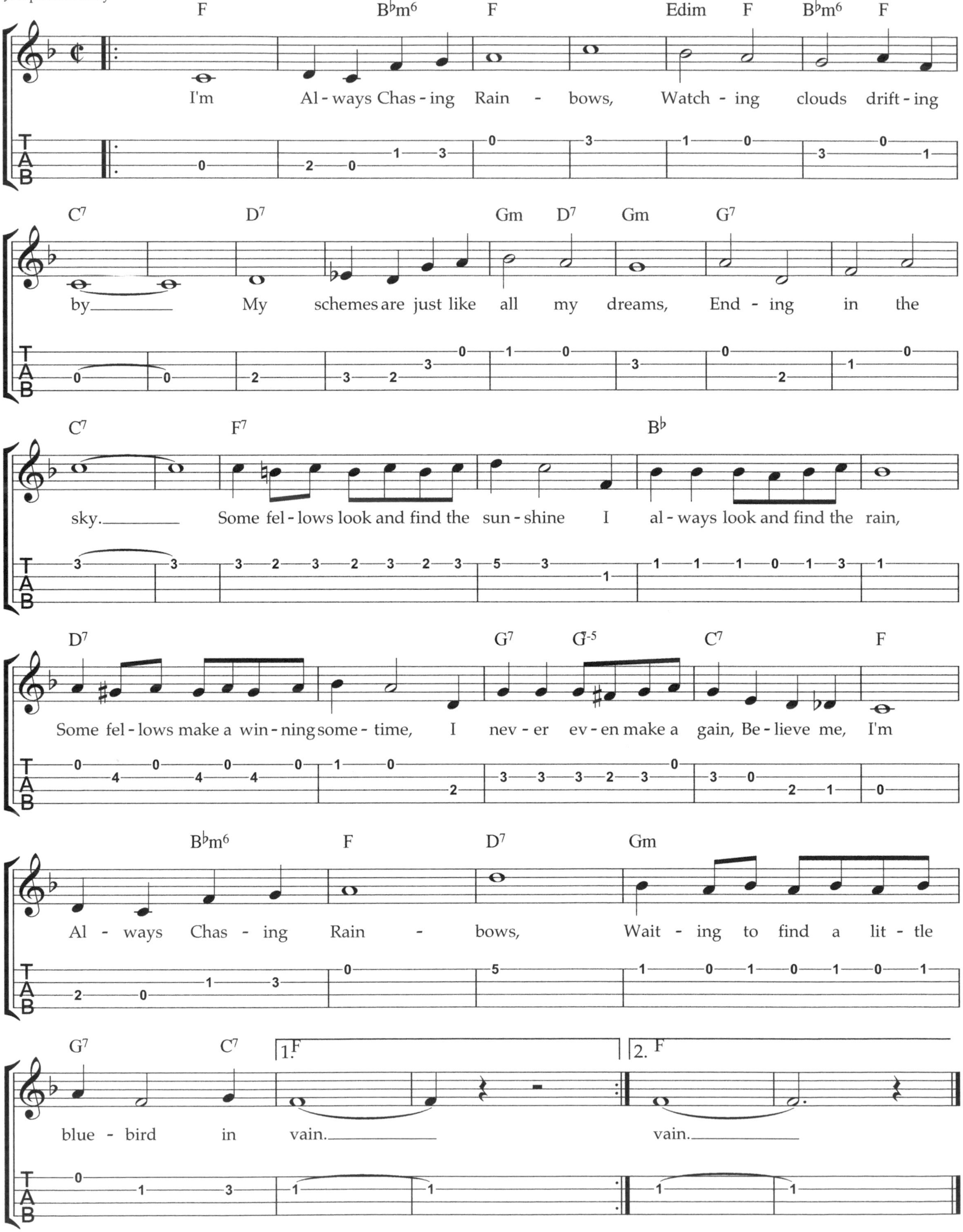
F B♭m6 F Edim F B♭m6 F
I'm Al - ways Chas - ing Rain - bows, Watch - ing clouds drift - ing
C7 D7 Gm D7 Gm G7
by My schemes are just like all my dreams, End - ing in the
C7 F7 B♭
sky. Some fel - lows look and find the sun - shine I al - ways look and find the rain,
D7 G7 G-5 C7 F
Some fel - lows make a win - ning some - time, I nev - er ev - en make a gain, Be - lieve me, I'm
B♭m6 F D7 Gm
Al - ways Chas - ing Rain - bows, Wait - ing to find a lit - tle
G7 C7 1.F 2. F
blue - bird in vain. vain.

I'm Sorry I Made You Cry

By N. J. Clesi
Arr. by Theodore Morse

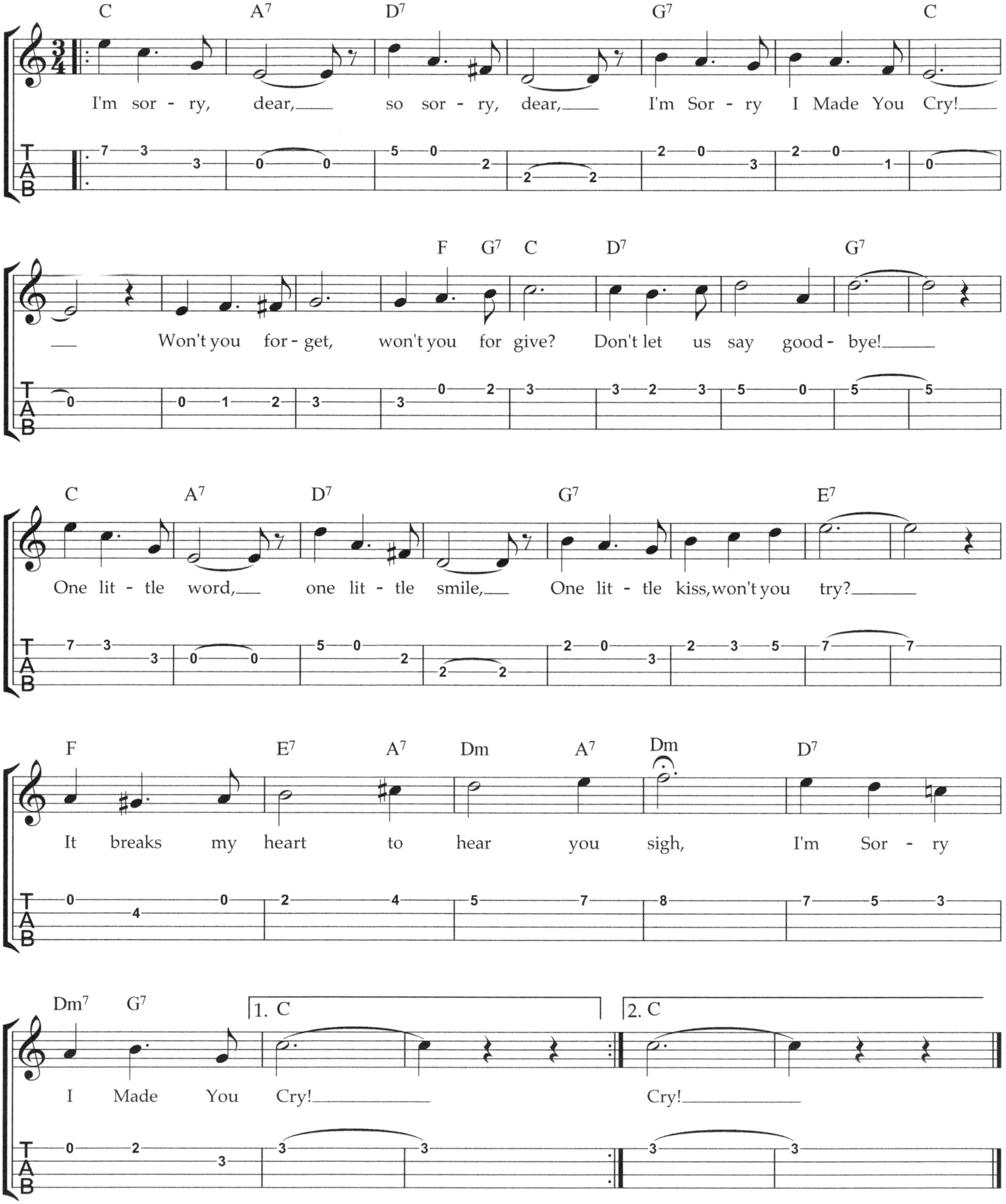
C A7 D7 G7 C
I'm sor - ry, dear, so sor - ry, dear, I'm Sor - ry I Made You Cry!
F G7 C D7 G7
Won't you for - get, won't you for give? Don't let us say good - bye!
C A7 D7 G7 E7
One lit - tle word, one lit - tle smile, One lit - tle kiss, won't you try?
F E7 A7 Dm A7 Dm D7
It breaks my heart to hear you sigh, I'm Sor - ry
Dm7 G7 1. C 2. C
I Made You Cry! Cry!

Ja-Da

Words and Music
by Bob Carleton

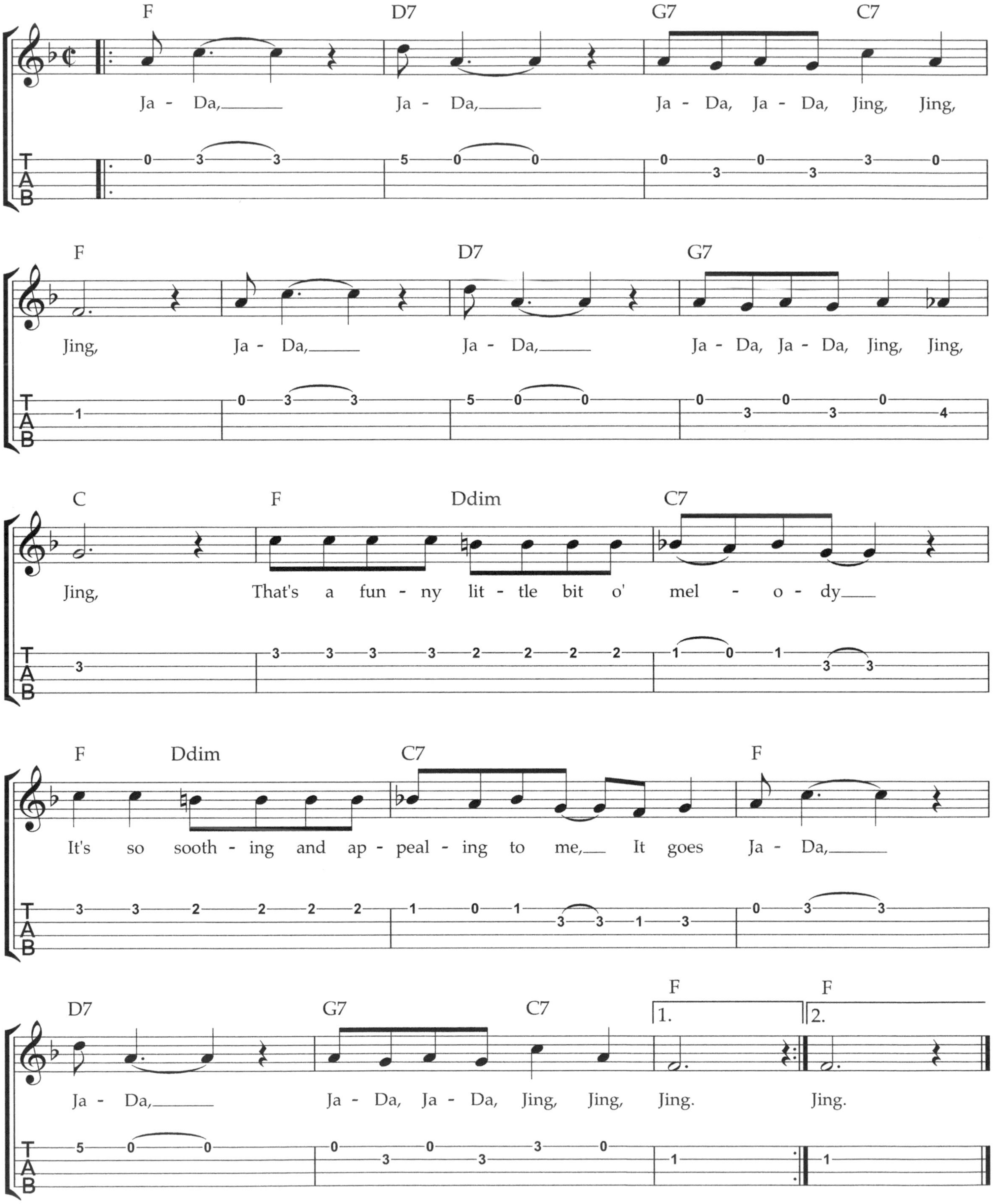
F D7 G7 C7
Ja - Da, Ja - Da, Ja - Da, Ja - Da, Jing, Jing,
F D7 G7
Jing, Ja - Da, Ja - Da, Ja - Da, Ja - Da, Jing, Jing,
C F Ddim C7
Jing, That's a fun - ny lit - tle bit o' mel - o - dy
F Ddim C7 F
It's so sooth - ing and ap - peal - ing to me, It goes Ja - Da,
D7 G7 C7 F F
1. 2.
Ja - Da, Ja - Da, Ja - Da, Jing, Jing, Jing. Jing.

Jeanie with the Light Brown Hair

Music by
Stephen Foster

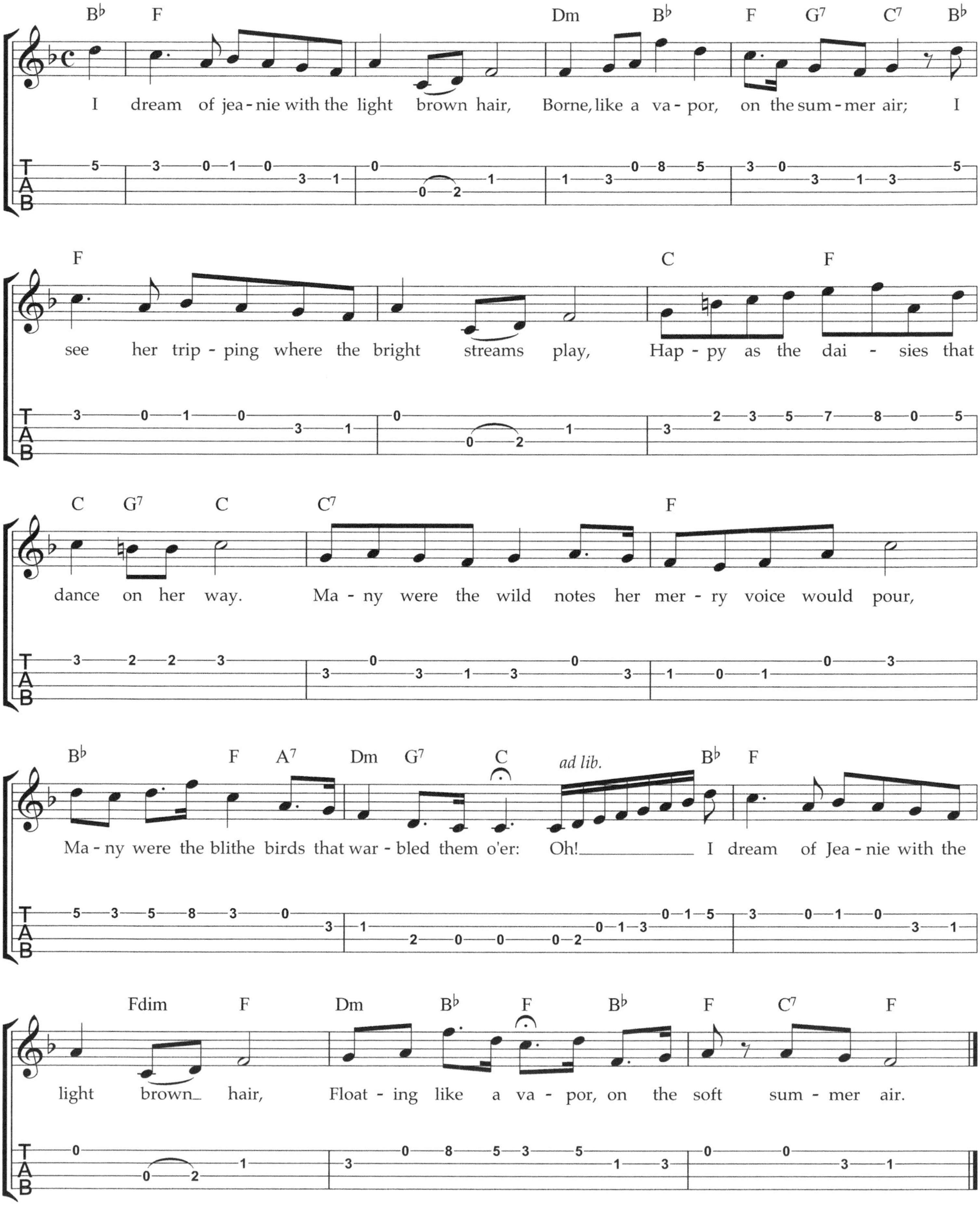
B♭ F Dm B♭ F G7 C7 B♭
I dream of jea - nie with the light brown hair, Borne, like a va - por, on the sum - mer air; I
F C F
see her trip - ping where the bright streams play, Hap - py as the dai - sies that
C G7 C C7 F
dance on her way. Ma - ny were the wild notes her mer - ry voice would pour,
B♭ F A7 Dm G7 C B♭ F
ad lib.
Ma - ny were the blithe birds that war - bled them o'er: Oh! I dream of Jea - nie with the
Fdim F Dm B♭ F B♭ F C7 F
light brown hair, Float - ing like a va - por, on the soft sum - mer air.

Ka Moae

Soloman Hiram

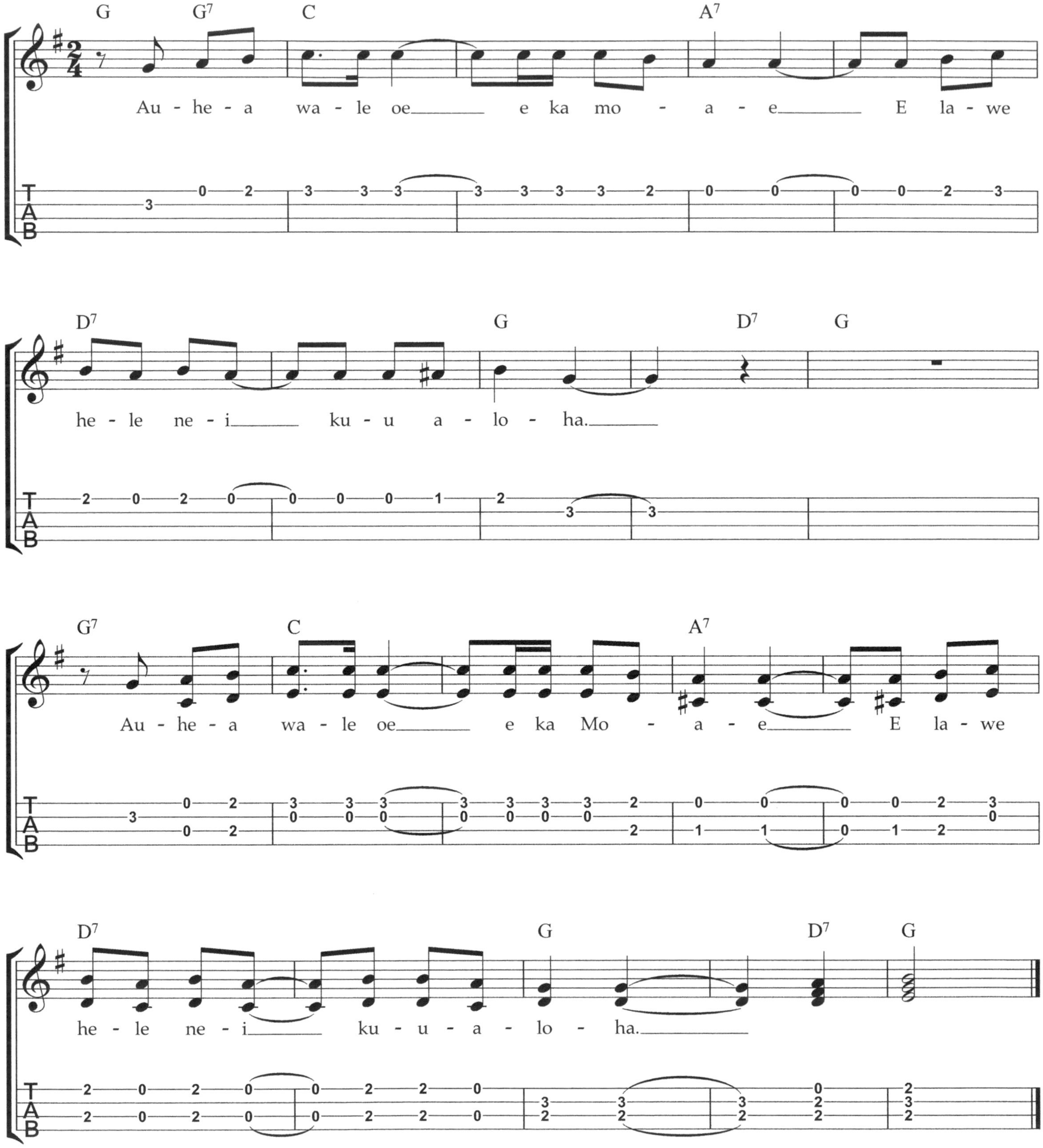
G G7 C A7
Au - he - a wa - le oe e ka mo - a - e E la - we
D7 G D7 G
he - le ne - i ku - u a - lo - ha.
G7 C A7
Au - he - a wa - le oe e ka Mo - a - e E la - we
D7 G D7 G
he - le ne - i ku - u - a - lo - ha.

Kaimana Hila

Chas. E. King

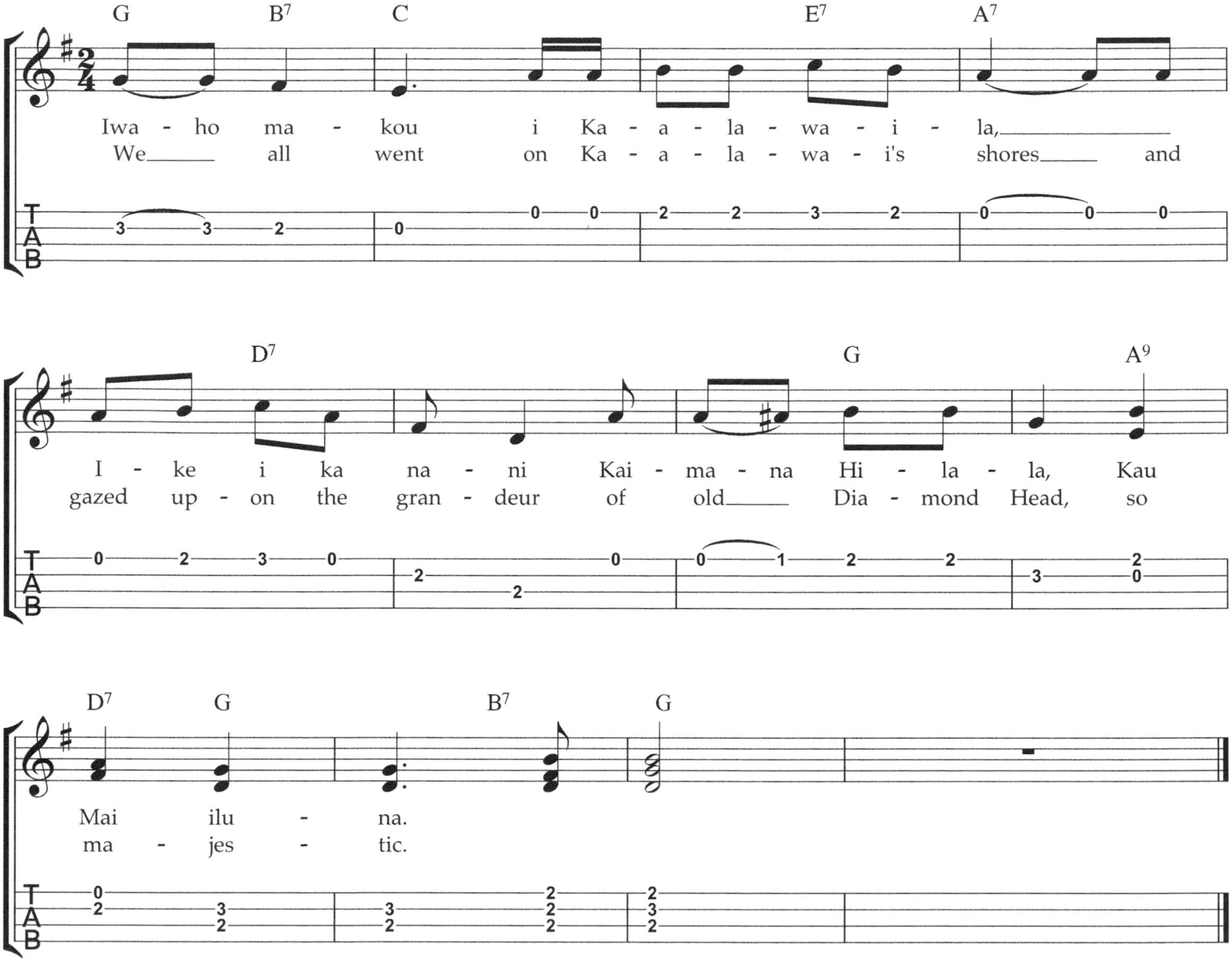
G B7 C E7 A7
Iwa - ho ma - kou i Ka - a - la - wa - i - la,
We all went on Ka - a - la - wa - i's shores and
D7 G A9
I - ke i ka na - ni Kai - ma - na Hi - la - la, Kau
gazed up - on the gran - deur of old Dia - mond Head, so
D7 G B7 G
Mai ilu - na.
ma - jes - tic.
TAB

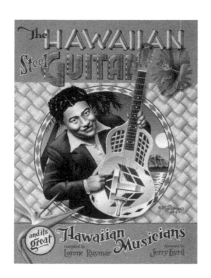

Ko Hanu Ka'u E Lia Nei

Chas. E. King

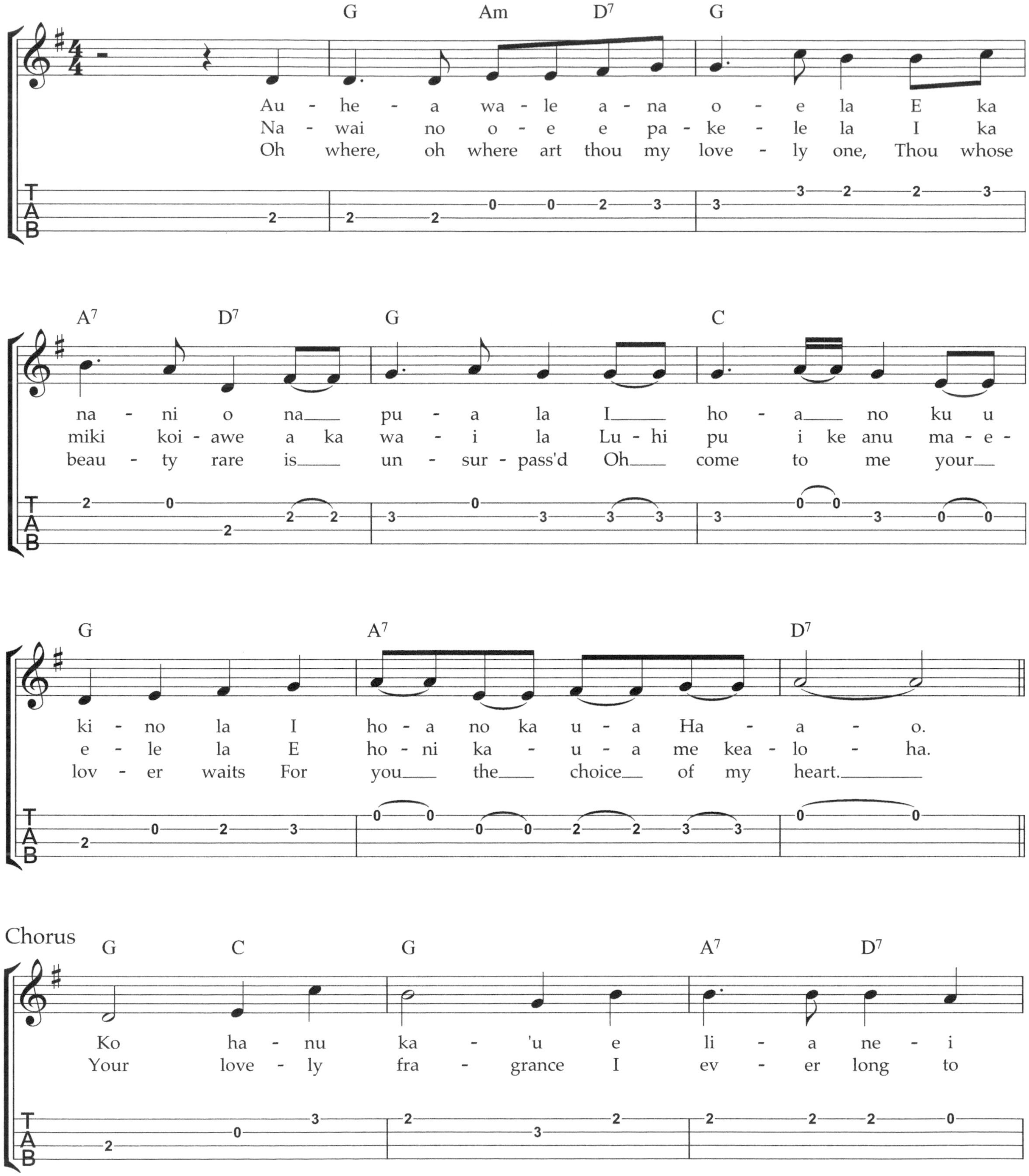
G Am D7 G
Au - he - a wa - le a - na o - e la E ka
Na - wai no o - e e pa - ke - le la I ka
Oh where, oh where art thou my love - ly one, Thou whose
A7 D7 G C
na - ni o na pu - a la I ho - a no ku u
miki koi - awe a ka wa - i la Lu - hi pu i ke anu ma - e -
beau - ty rare is un - sur - pass'd Oh come to me your
G A7 D7
ki - no la I ho - a no ka u - a Ha - a - o.
e - le la E ho - ni ka - u - a me kea - lo - ha.
lov - er waits For you the choice of my heart.
Chorus
G C G A7 D7
Ko ha - nu ka - 'u e li - a ne - i
Your love - ly fra - grance I ev - er long to
TAB

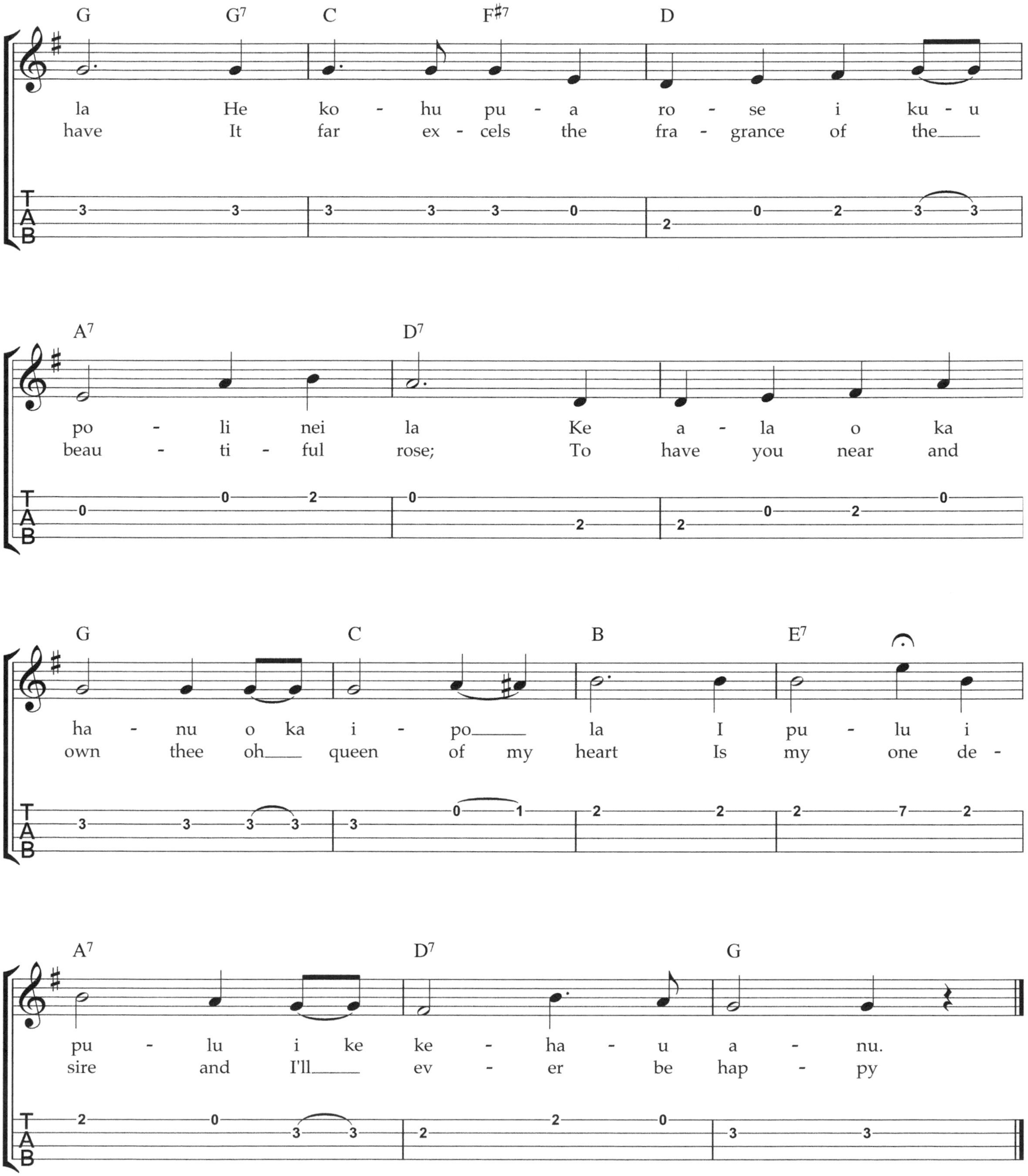
G G7 C F♯7 D
la He ko - hu pu - a ro - se i ku - u
have It far ex - cels the fra - grance of the
A7 D7
po - li nei la Ke a - la o ka
beau - ti - ful rose; To have you near and
G C B E7
ha - nu o ka i - po la I pu - lu i
own thee oh queen of my heart Is my one de -
A7 D7 G
pu - lu i ke ke - ha - u a - nu.
sire and I'll ev - er be hap - py

Koni Au I Ka Wai

King Kalakaua
Arranged by Chas. E. King

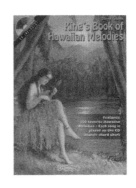

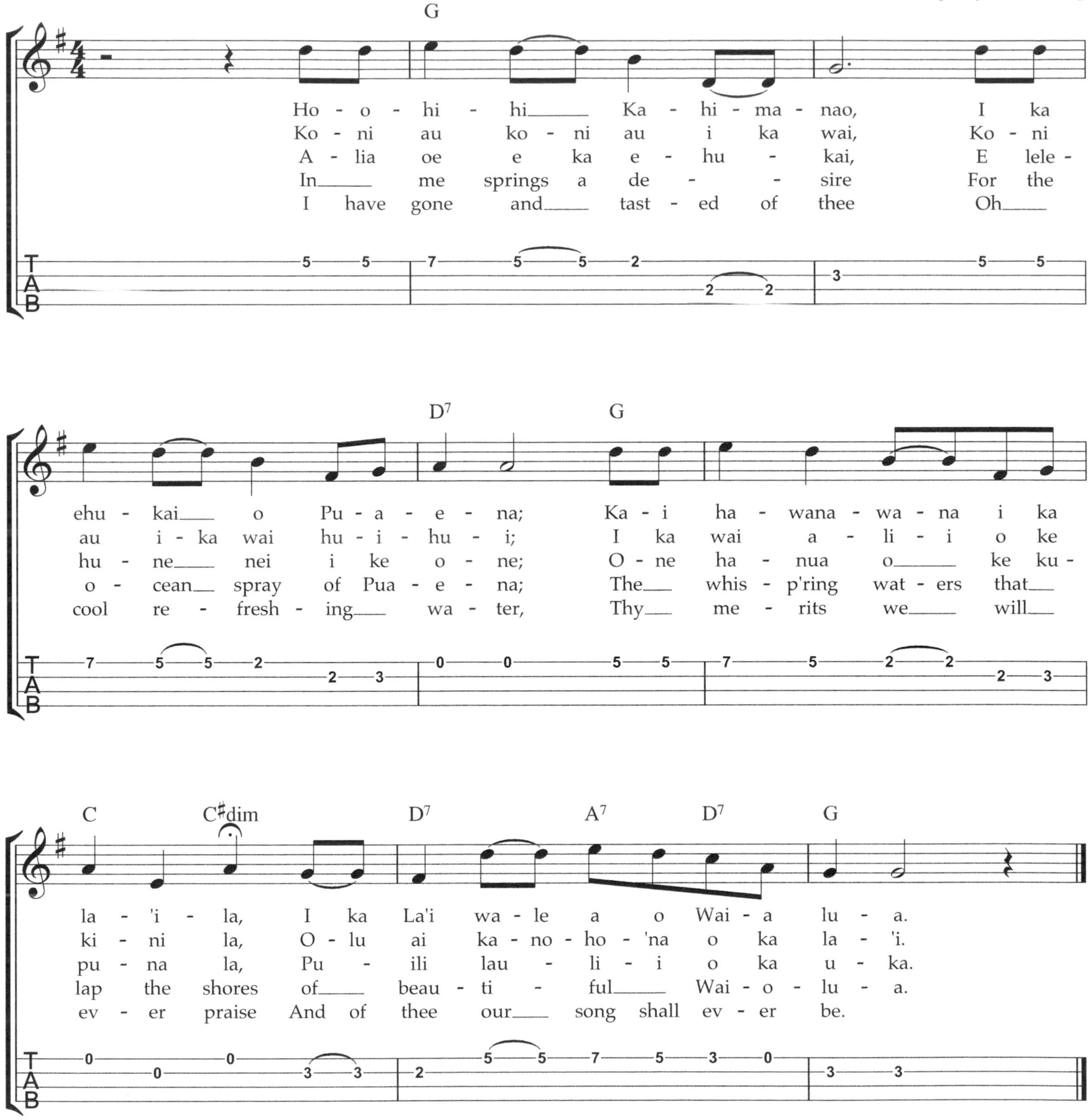
G
Ho - o - hi - hi Ka - hi - ma - nao, I ka
Ko - ni au ko - ni au i ka wai, Ko - ni
A - lia oe e ka e - hu - kai, E lele -
In me springs a de - - sire For the
I have gone and tast - ed of thee Oh
T
A
B
D7 G
ehu - kai o Pu - a - e - na; Ka - i ha - wana - wa - na i ka
au i - ka wai hu - i - hu - i; I ka wai a - li - i o ke
hu - ne nei i ke o - ne; O - ne ha - nua o ke ku -
o - cean spray of Pua - e - na; The whis - p'ring wat - ers that
cool re - fresh - ing wa - ter, Thy me - rits we will
C C♯dim D7 A7 D7 G
la - 'i - la, I ka La'i wa - le a o Wai - a lu - a.
ki - ni la, O - lu ai ka - no - ho - 'na o ka la - 'i.
pu - na la, Pu - ili lau - li - i o ka u - ka.
lap the shores of beau - ti - ful Wai - o - lu - a.
ev - er praise And of thee our song shall ev - er be.

Lei Lehua O Panaewa

Words Anonymoous
Chas. E. King

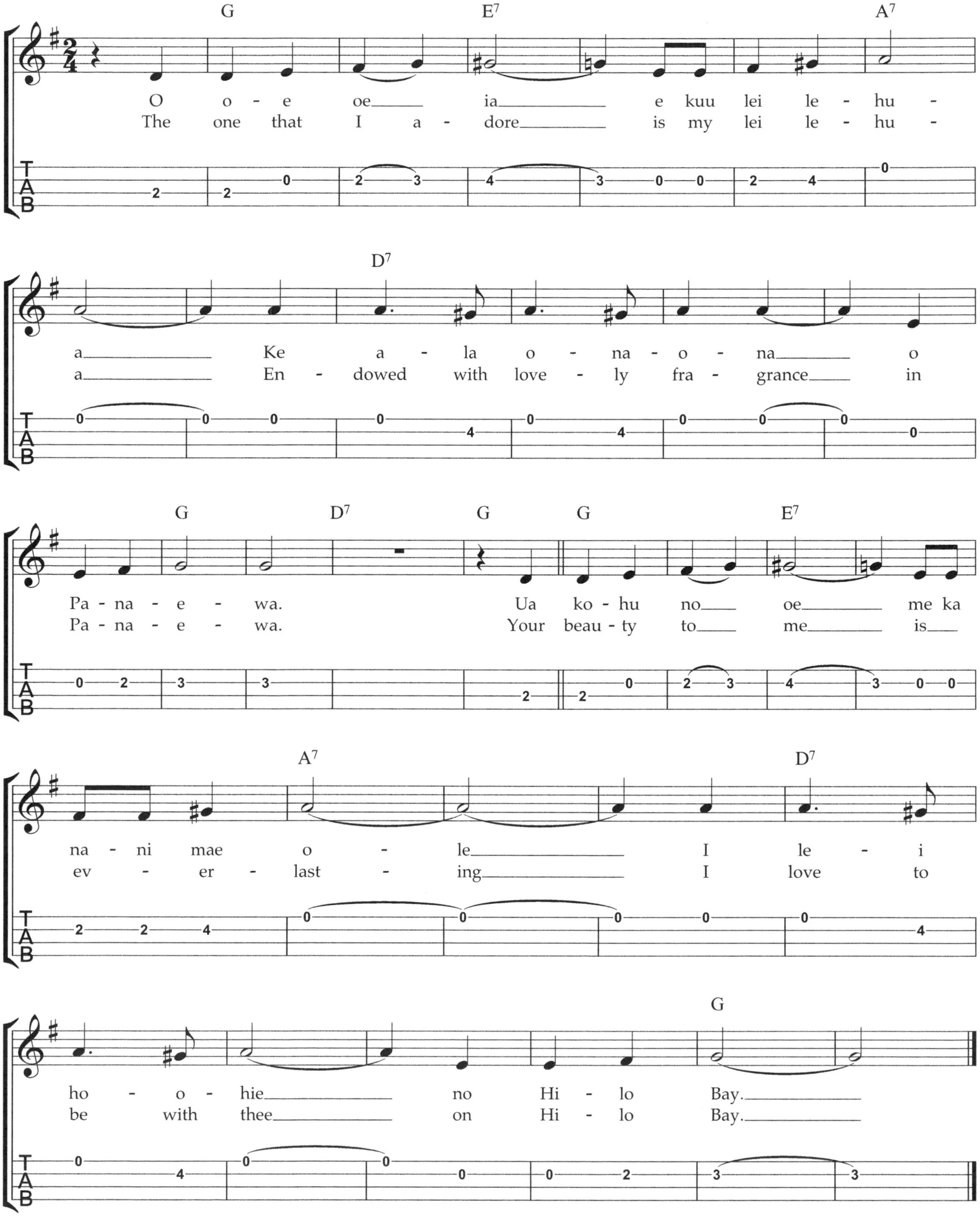
G E7 A7
O o - e oe ia e kuu lei le - hu -
The one that I a - dore is my lei le - hu -
D7
a Ke a - la o - na - o - na o
a En - dowed with love - ly fra - grance in
G D7 G G E7
Pa - na - e - wa. Ua ko - hu no oe me ka
Pa - na - e - wa. Your beau - ty to me is
A7 D7
na - ni mae o - le I le - i
ev - er - last - ing I love to
G
ho - o - hie no Hi - lo Bay.
be with thee on Hi - lo Bay.

Linger Awhile

Lyrics by
Harry Owens

Music by
Vincent Rose

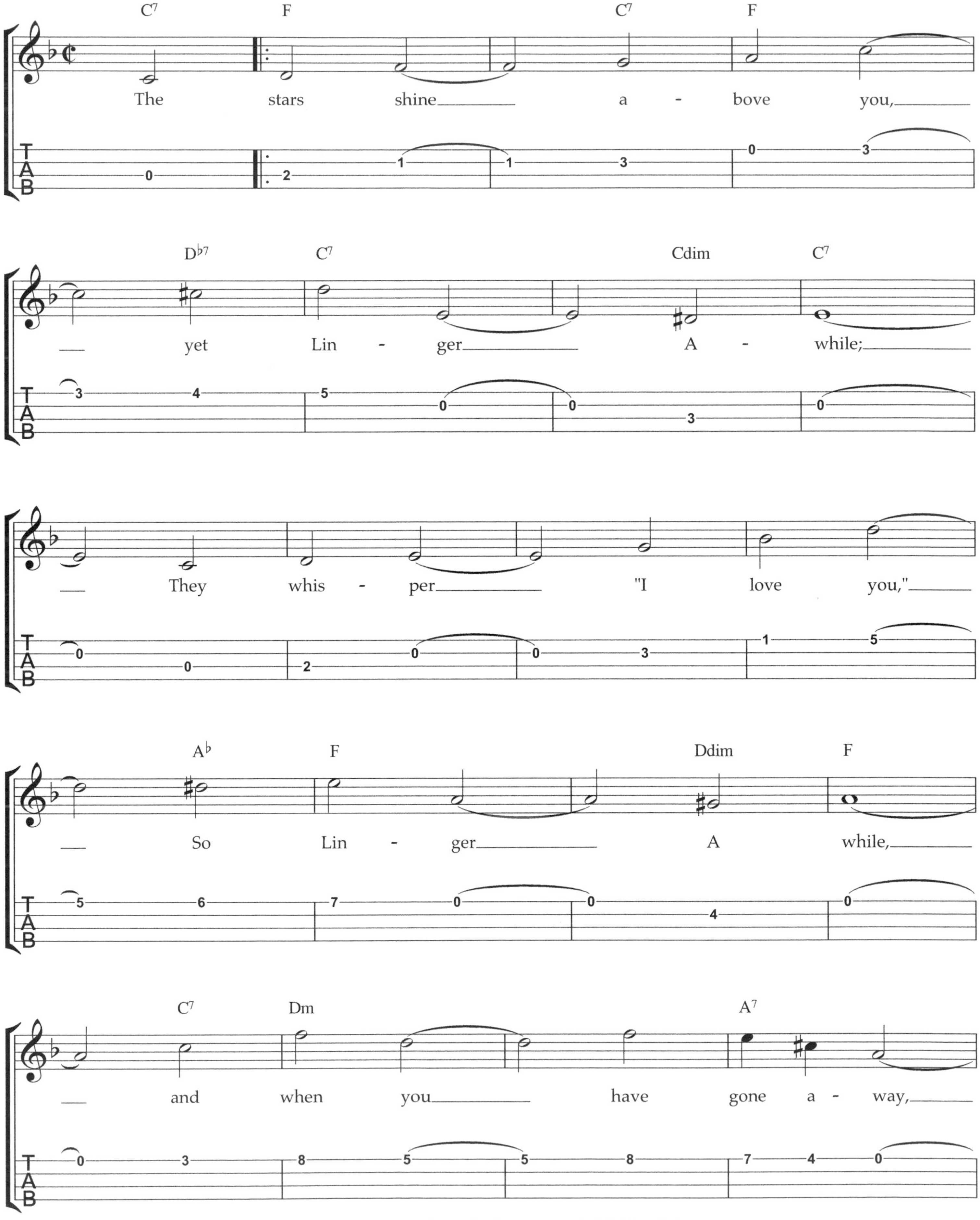
C7 F C7 F
The stars shine a - bove you,
Db7 C7 Cdim C7
yet Lin - ger A - while;
They whis - per "I love you,"
Ab F Ddim F
So Lin - ger A while,
C7 Dm A7
and when you have gone a - way,
T
A
B
0 2 1 1 3 0 3
3 4 5 0 0 3 0
0 0 2 0 0 3 1 5
5 6 7 0 0 4 0
0 3 8 5 5 8 7 4 0

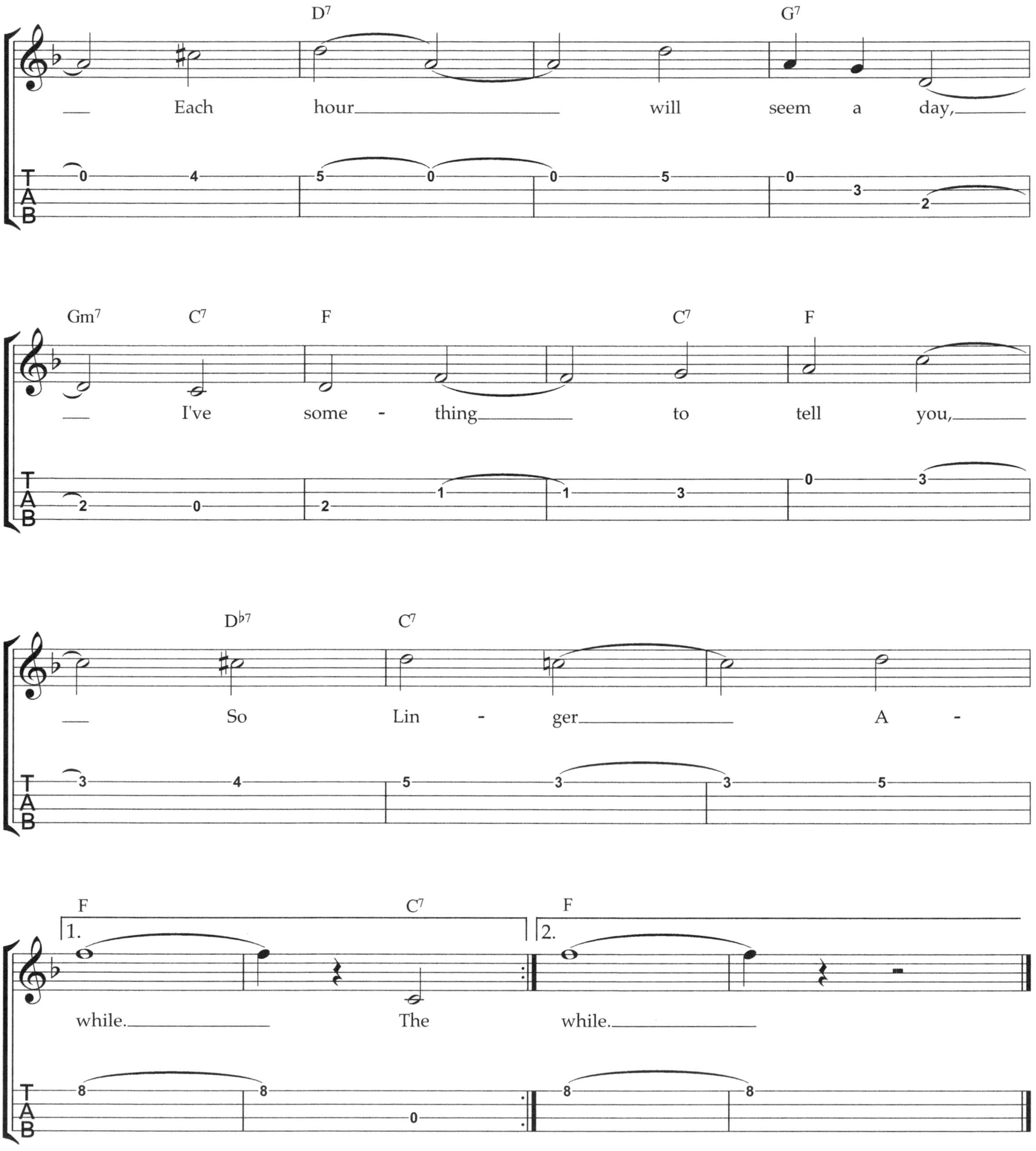
D7 G7
Each hour will seem a day,
Gm7 C7 F C7 F
I've some - thing to tell you,
D♭7 C7
So Lin - ger A -
F C7 F
1. 2.
while. The while.

Maikai Waipio

Princess Likelike

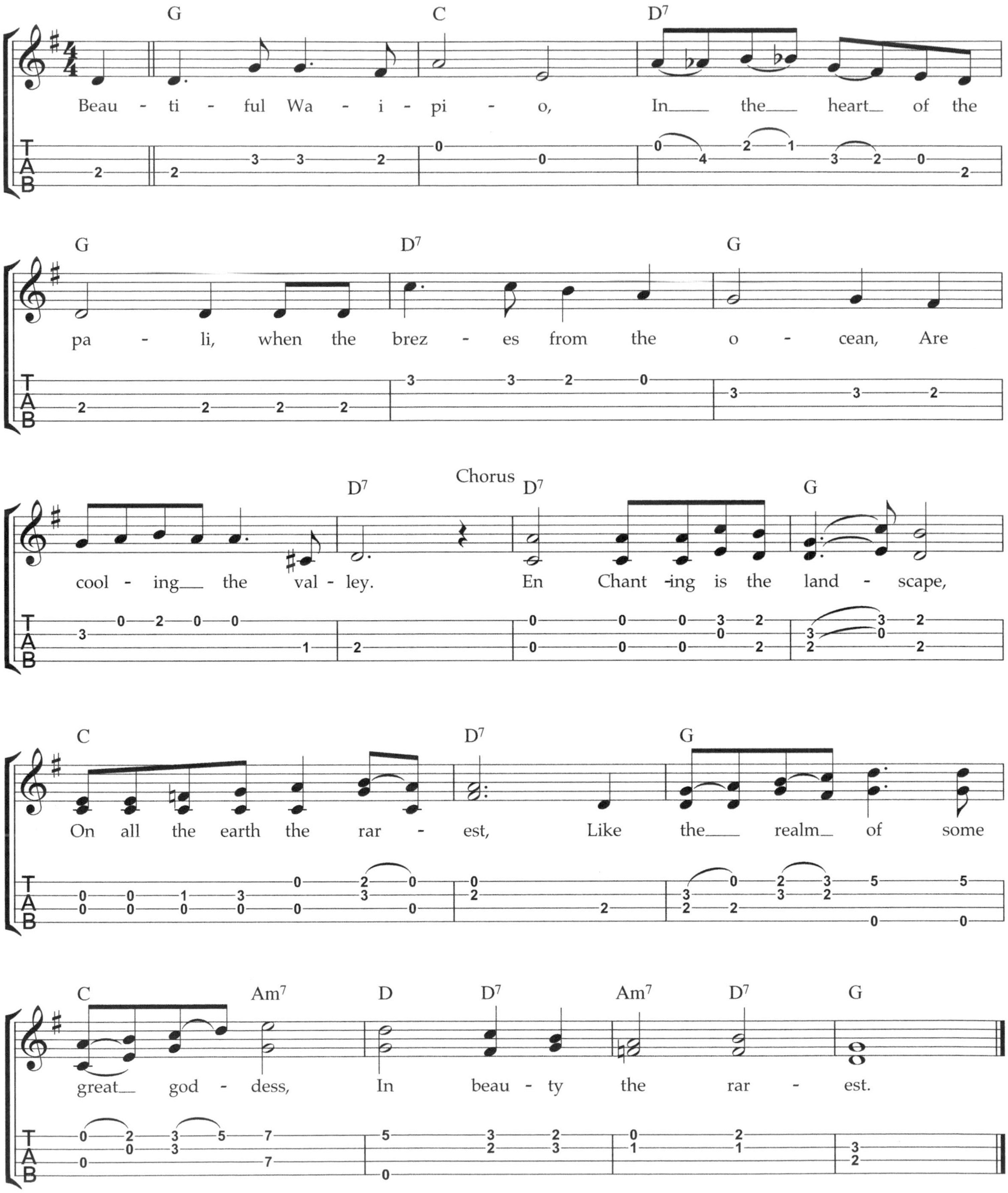
G C D7
Beau - ti - ful Wa - i - pi - o, In the heart of the
G D7 G
pa - li, when the brez - es from the o - cean, Are
D7 Chorus D7 G
cool - ing the val - ley. En Chant -ing is the land - scape,
C D7 G
On all the earth the rar - est, Like the realm of some
C Am7 D D7 Am7 D7 G
great god - dess, In beau - ty the rar - est.

Moani Ke Ala

Prince leleiohoku
Arranged by Chas. E. King

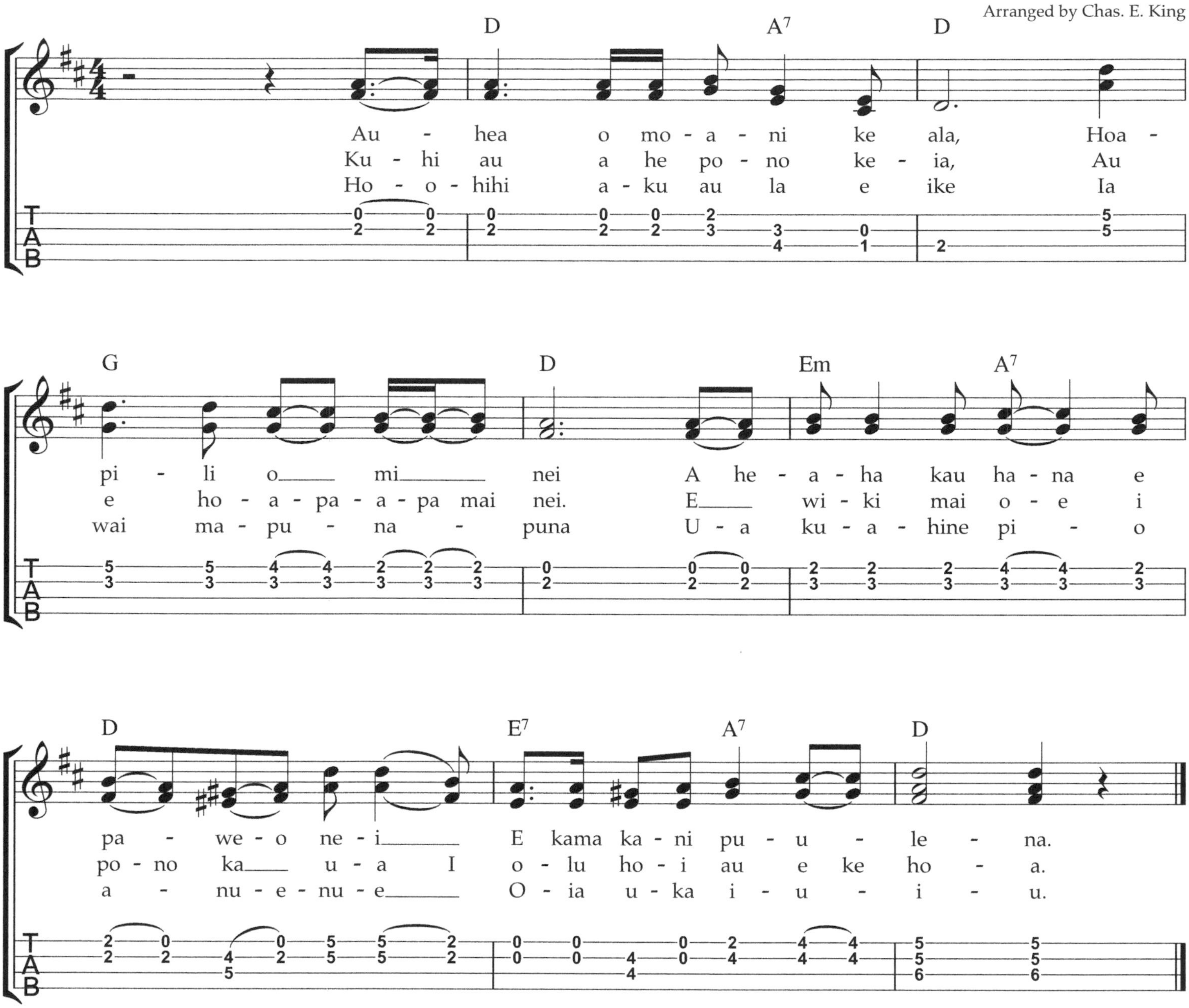
D A7 D
Au - hea o mo - a - ni ke ala, Hoa -
Ku - hi au a he po - no ke - ia, Au
Ho - o - hihi a - ku au la e ike Ia
G D Em A7
pi - li o mi nei A he - a - ha kau ha - na e
e ho - a - pa - a - pa mai nei. E wi - ki mai o - e i
wai ma - pu - na - puna U - a ku - a - hine pi - o
D E7 A7 D
pa - we - o ne - i E kama ka - ni pu - u - le - na.
po - no ka u - a I o - lu ho - i au e ke ho - a.
a - nu - e - nu - e O - ia u - ka i - u - i - u.

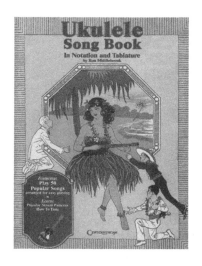

My Dear Hawaii

Chas. E. King

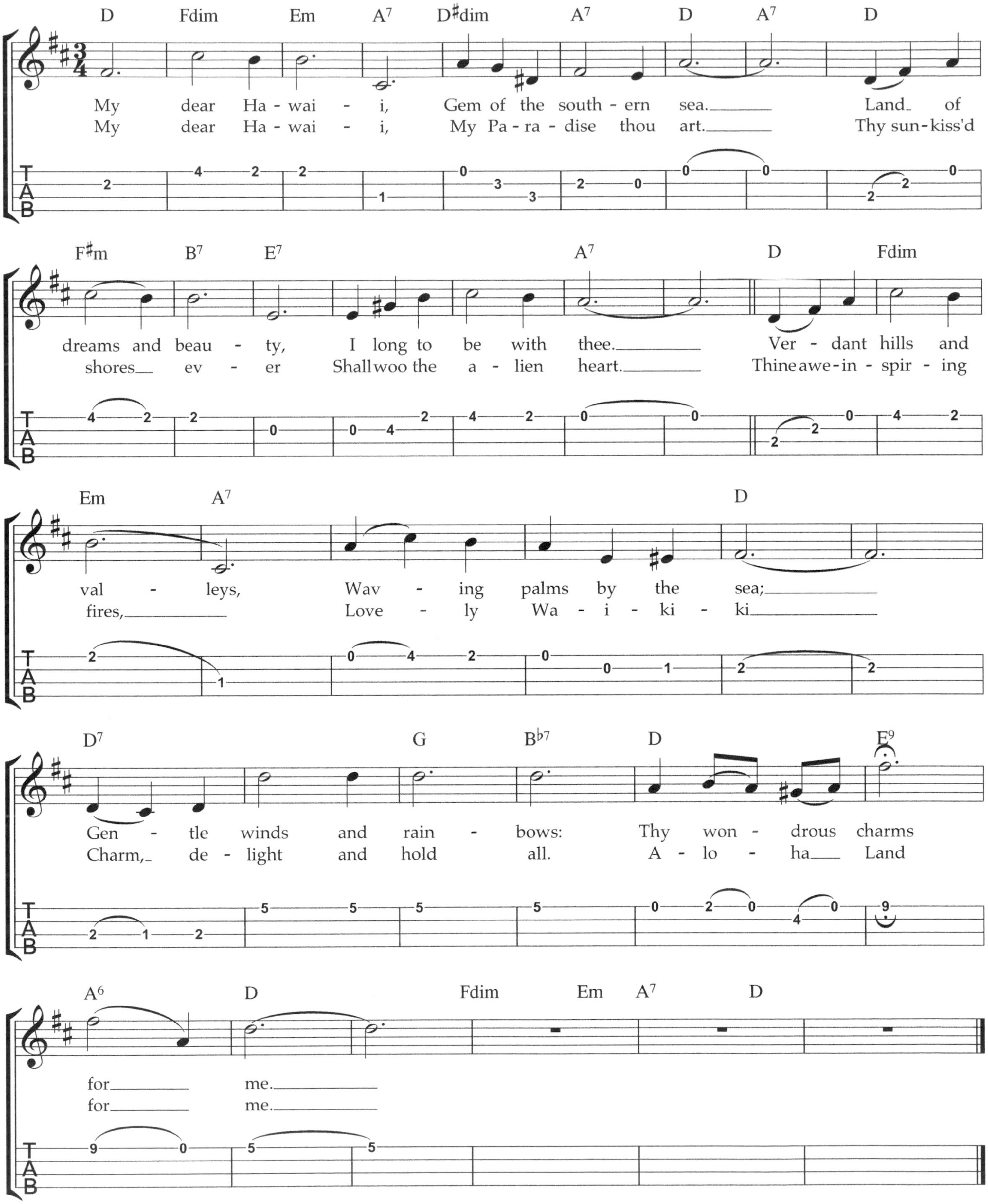
D Fdim Em A7 D♯dim A7 D A7 D
My dear Ha - wai - i, Gem of the south - ern sea. Land of
My dear Ha - wai - i, My Pa - ra - dise thou art. Thy sun-kiss'd
F♯m B7 E7 A7 D Fdim
dreams and beau - ty, I long to be with thee. Ver - dant hills and
shores ev - er Shall woo the a - lien heart. Thine awe - in - spir - ing
Em A7 D
val - leys, Wav - ing palms by the sea;
fires, Love - ly Wa - i - ki - ki
D7 G B♭7 D E9
Gen - tle winds and rain - bows: Thy won - drous charms
Charm, de - light and hold all. A - lo - ha Land
A6 D Fdim Em A7 D
for me.
for me.

Nelly Was a Lady

Music by
Stephen Foster

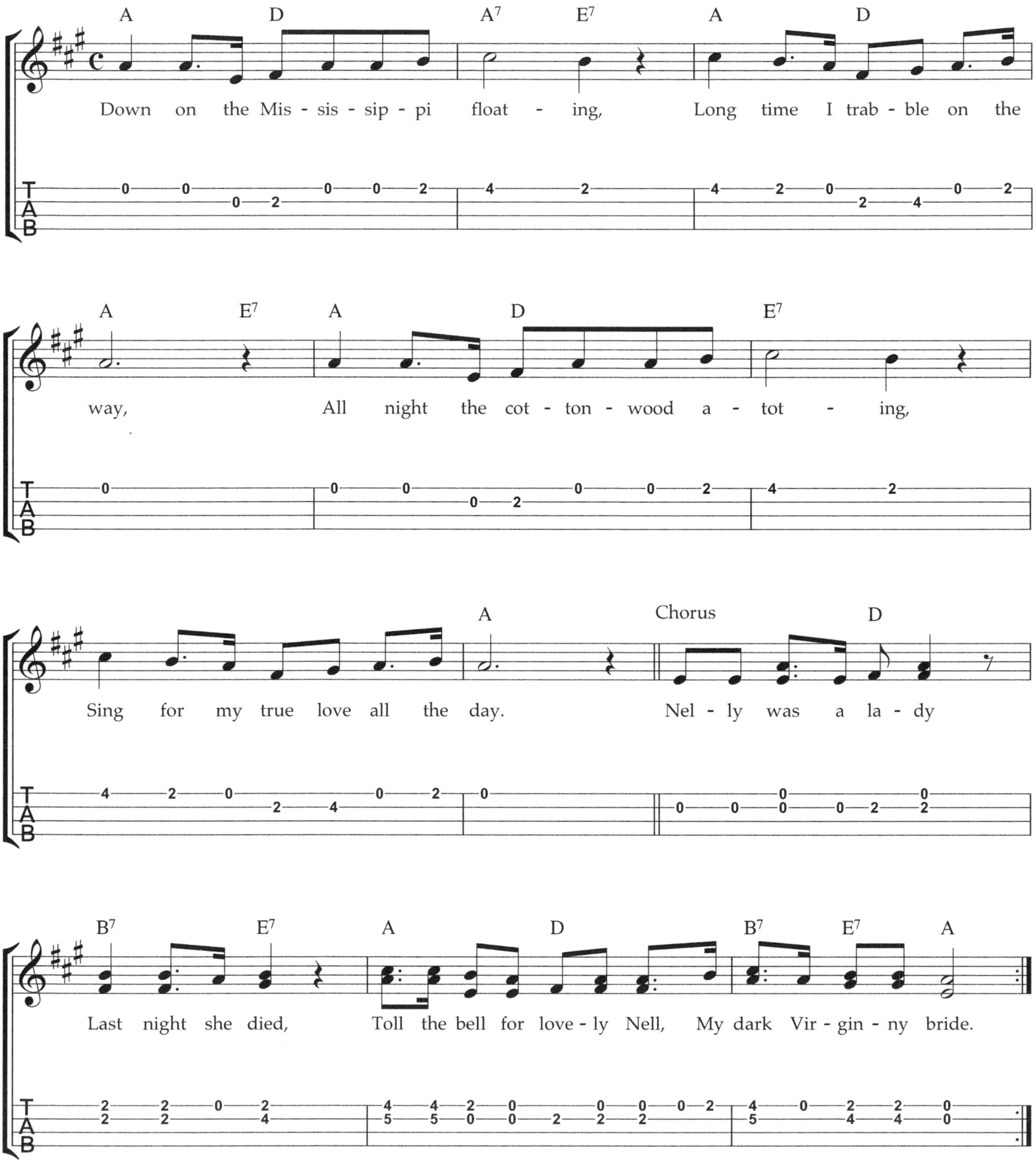

Down on the Mis - sis - sip - pi float - ing, Long time I trab - ble on the
way, All night the cot - ton - wood a - tot - ing,
Sing for my true love all the day.
Chorus
Nel - ly was a la - dy
Last night she died, Toll the bell for love - ly Nell, My dark Vir - gin - ny bride.

No, No, Nora

Words by
Gus Khan

Music by Ted Fiorito
and Ernie Erdman

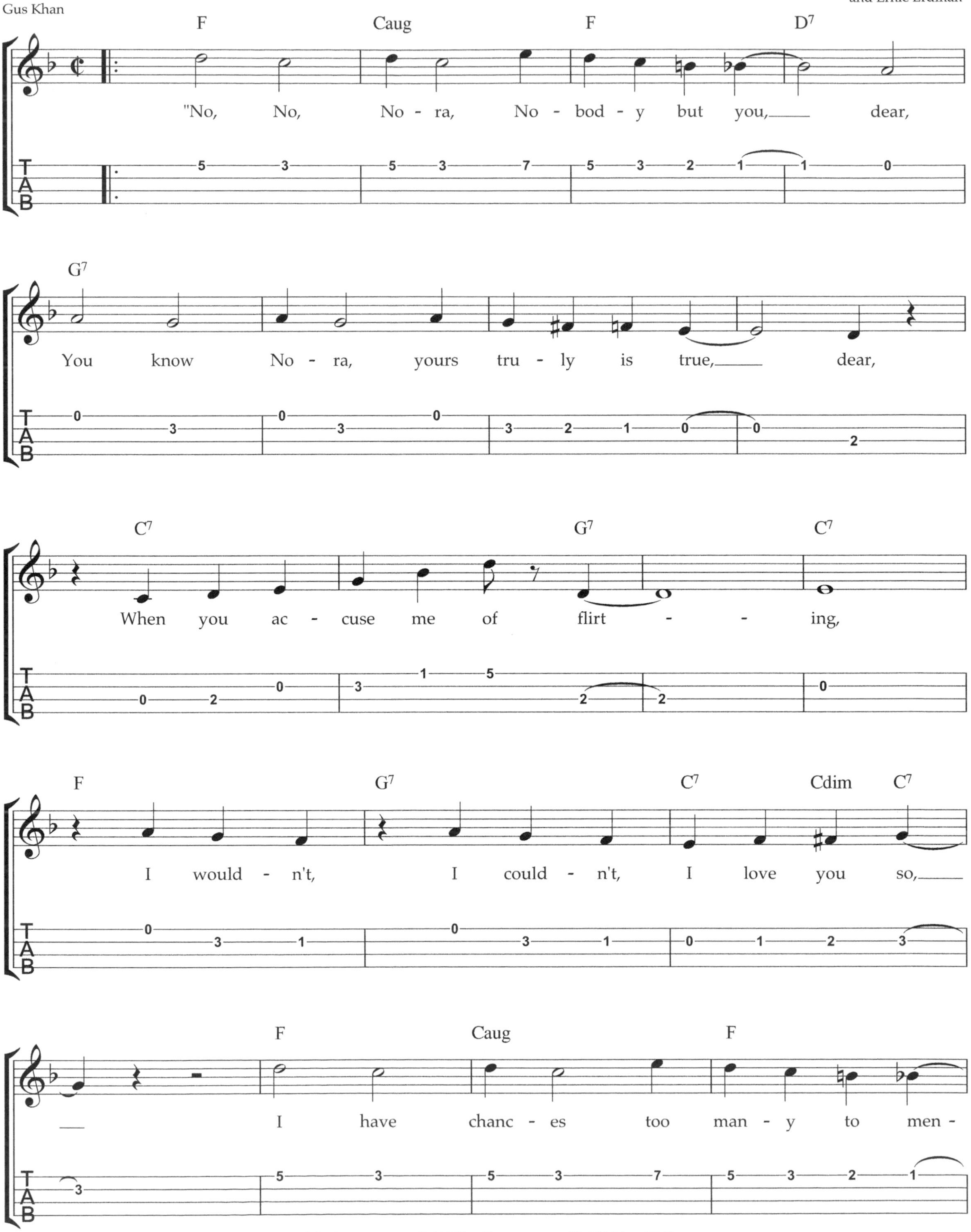
F Caug F D7
"No, No, No - ra, No - bod - y but you, dear,
G7
You know No - ra, yours tru - ly is true, dear,
C7 G7 C7
When you ac - cuse me of flirt - - ing,
F G7 C7 Cdim C7
I would - n't, I could - n't, I love you so,
F Caug F
I have chanc - es too man - y to men -

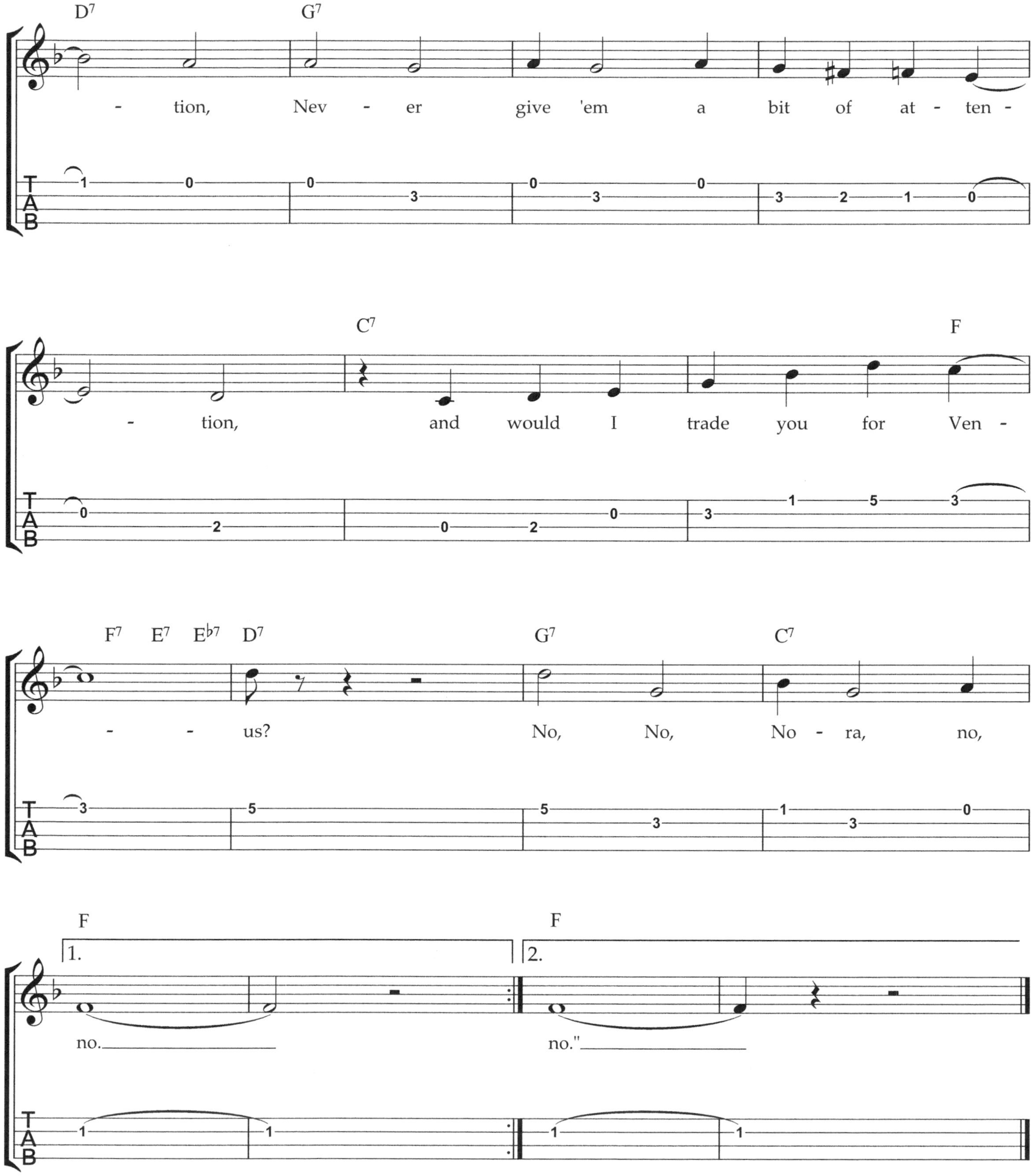
D7 G7
- tion, Nev - er give 'em a bit of at - ten -
C7 F
- tion, and would I trade you for Ven -
F7 E7 E♭7 D7 G7 C7
- - us? No, No, No - ra, no,
F 1. F 2.
no.
no."

The Old Chisholm Trail

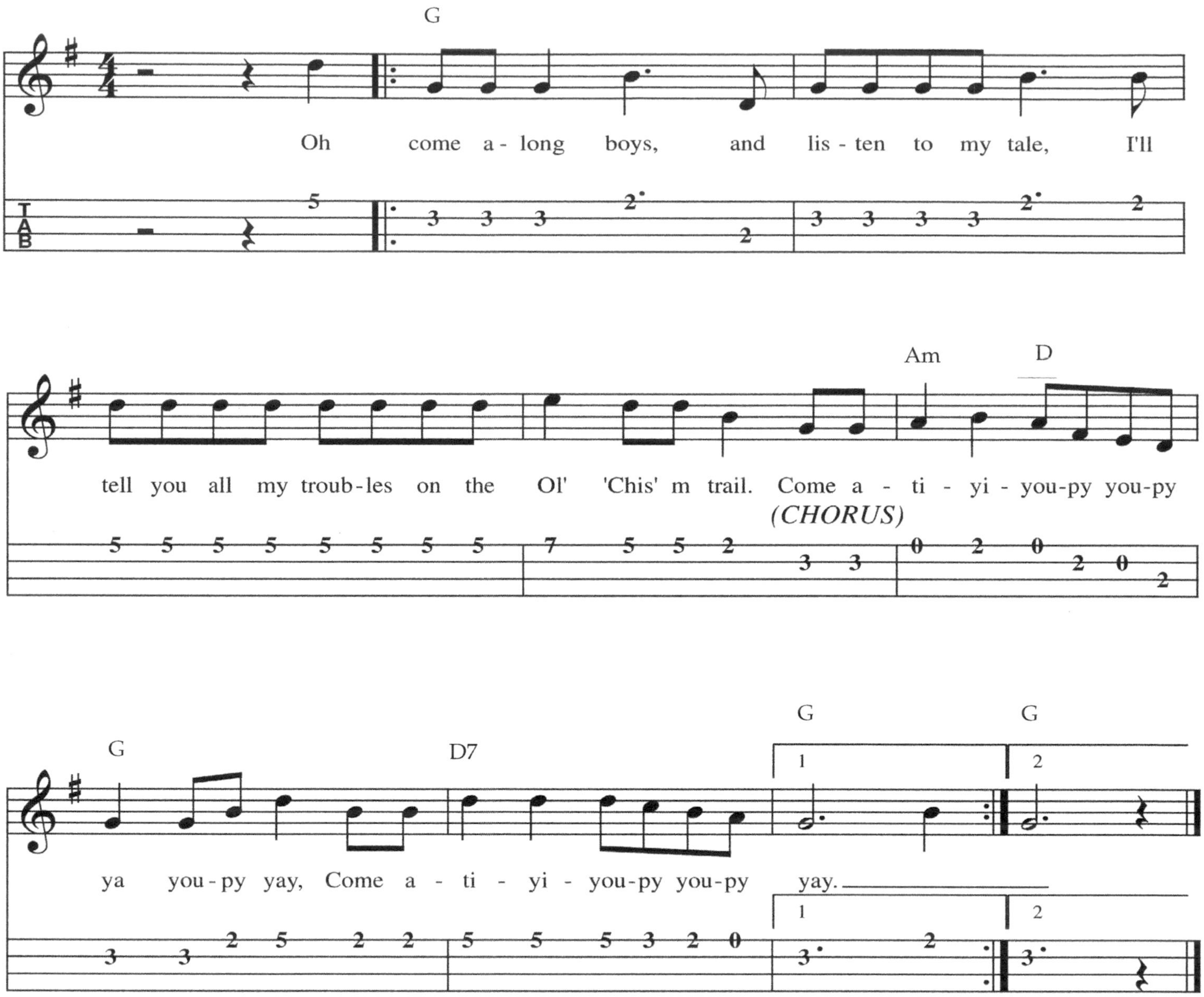
G
Oh come a-long boys, and lis-ten to my tale, I'll
Am D
tell you all my troub-les on the Ol' 'Chis' m trail. Come a - ti - yi - you-py you-py
(CHORUS)
G D7 G G
1 2
ya you-py yay, Come a - ti - yi - you-py you-py yay.

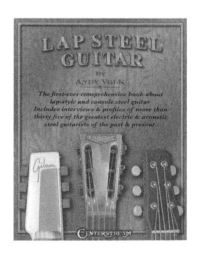

Old Folks at Home

Music by
Stephen Foster

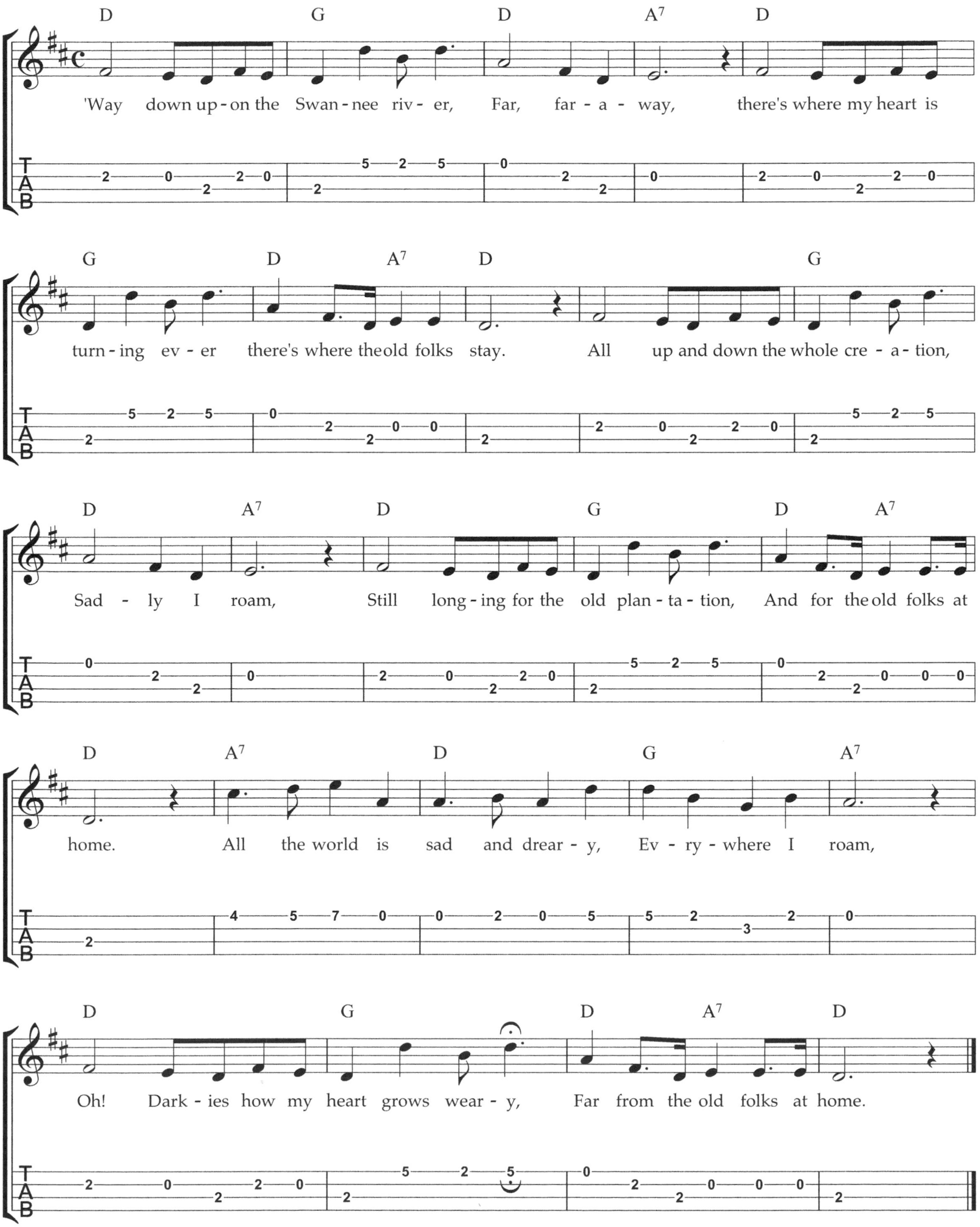
D G D A7 D
'Way down up-on the Swan-nee riv-er, Far, far-a-way, there's where my heart is
G D A7 D G
turn-ing ev-er there's where the old folks stay. All up and down the whole cre-a-tion,
D A7 D G D A7
Sad-ly I roam, Still long-ing for the old plan-ta-tion, And for the old folks at
D A7 D G A7
home. All the world is sad and drear-y, Ev-ry-where I roam,
D G D A7 D
Oh! Dark-ies how my heart grows wear-y, Far from the old folks at home.

Old Paint

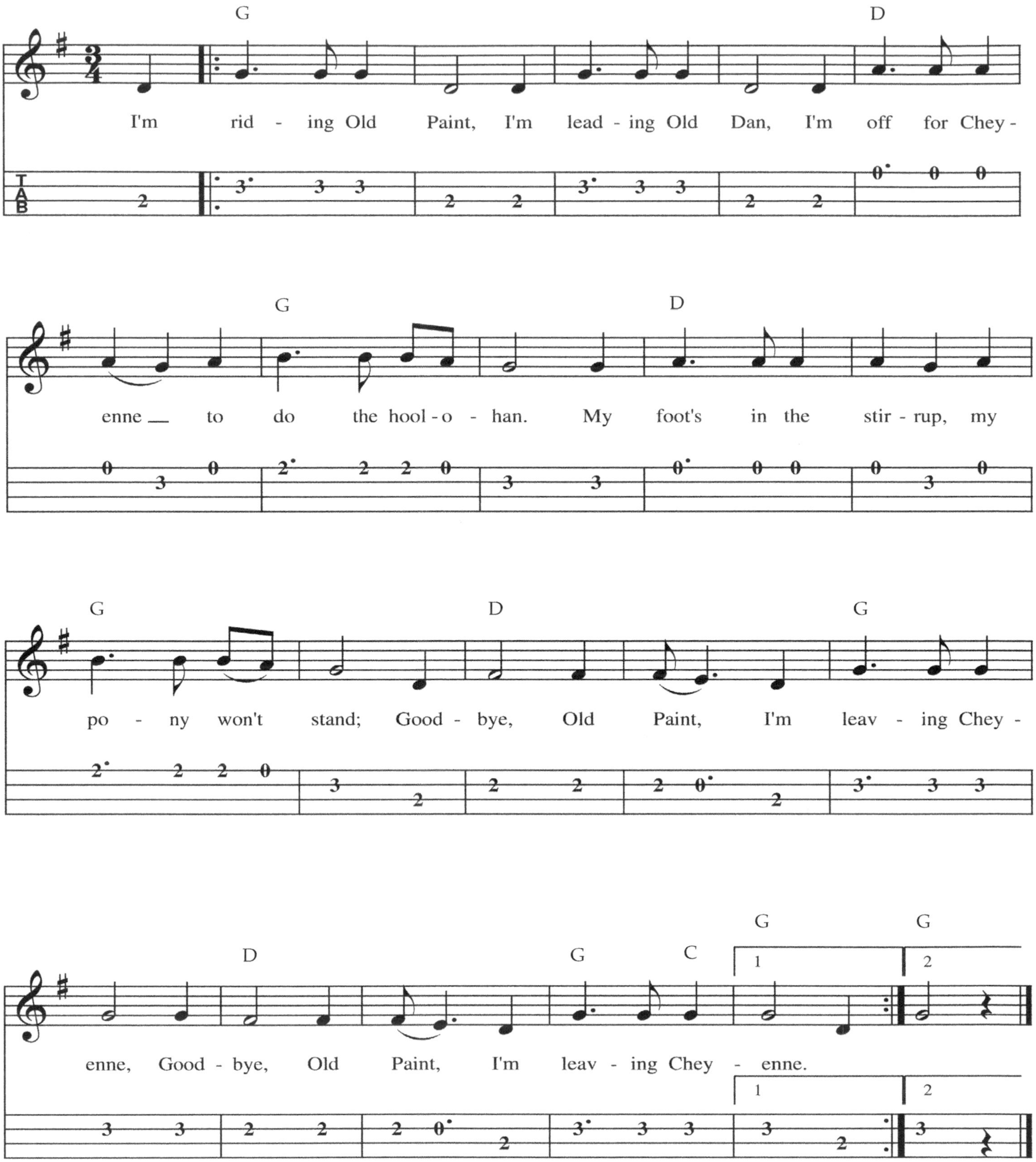
G D
I'm rid - ing Old Paint, I'm lead - ing Old Dan, I'm off for Chey -
G D
enne to do the hool - o - han. My foot's in the stir - rup, my
G D G
po - ny won't stand; Good - bye, Old Paint, I'm leav - ing Chey -
D G C G G
1 2
enne, Good - bye, Old Paint, I'm leav - ing Chey - enne.
TAB

Peg O' My Heart

Words by
Alfred Bryan

Music by
Fred Fisher

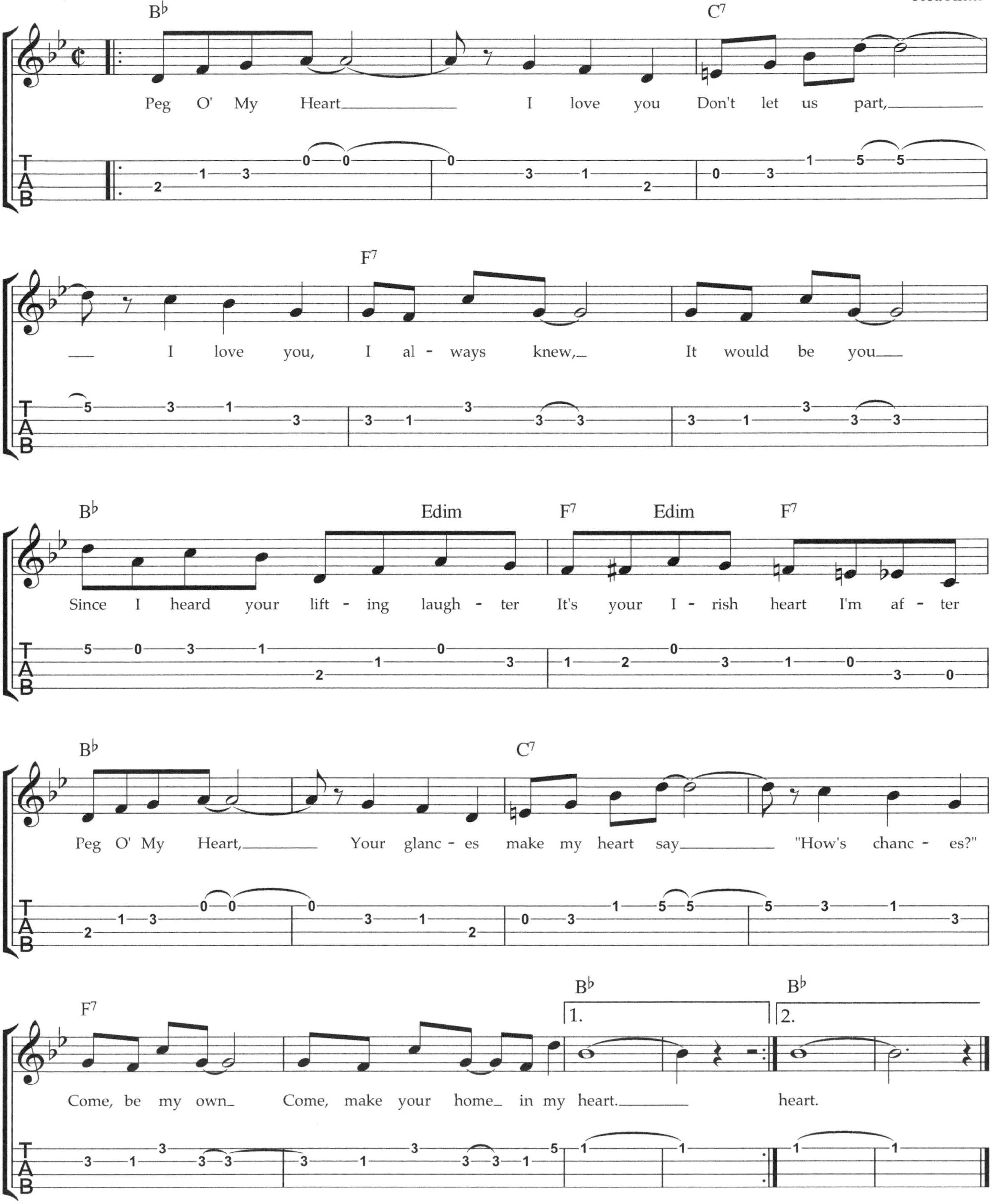
Bb C7
Peg O' My Heart I love you Don't let us part,
F7
I love you, I al - ways knew, It would be you
Bb Edim F7 Edim F7
Since I heard your lift - ing laugh - ter It's your I - rish heart I'm af - ter
Bb C7
Peg O' My Heart, Your glanc - es make my heart say "How's chanc - es?"
F7 Bb Bb
1. 2.
Come, be my own Come, make your home in my heart. heart.

Poli Pumehana

David Nape
James Kaahiki

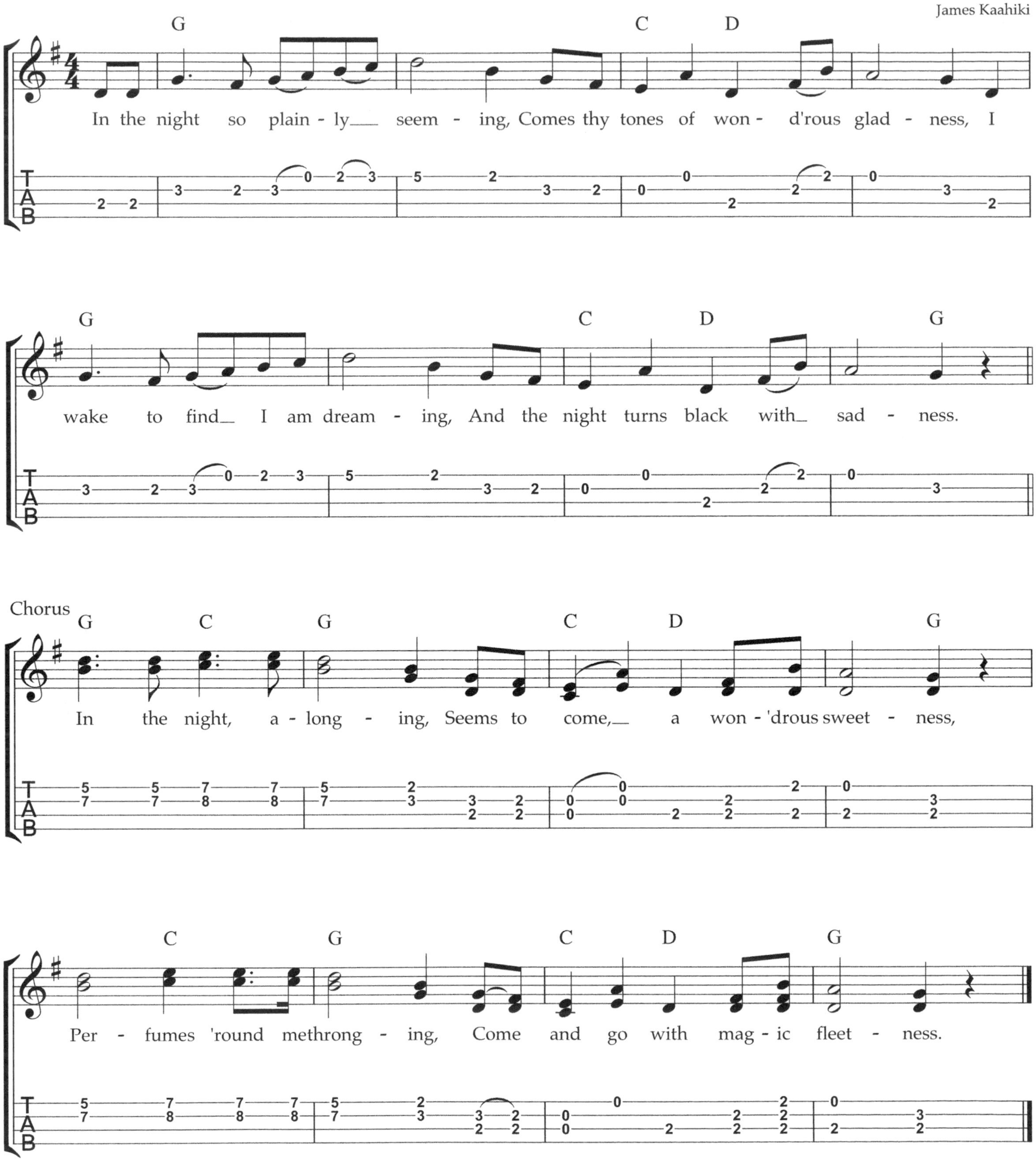
G C D
In the night so plain - ly___ seem - ing, Comes thy tones of won - d'rous glad - ness, I
G C D G
wake to find__ I am dream - ing, And the night turns black with__ sad - ness.
Chorus
G C G C D G
In the night, a - long - ing, Seems to come,__ a won - 'drous sweet - ness,
C G C D G
Per - fumes 'round me throng - ing, Come and go with mag - ic fleet - ness.

The Sidewalks Of New York

Words by
Charles B. Lawler

Music by
James W. Blake

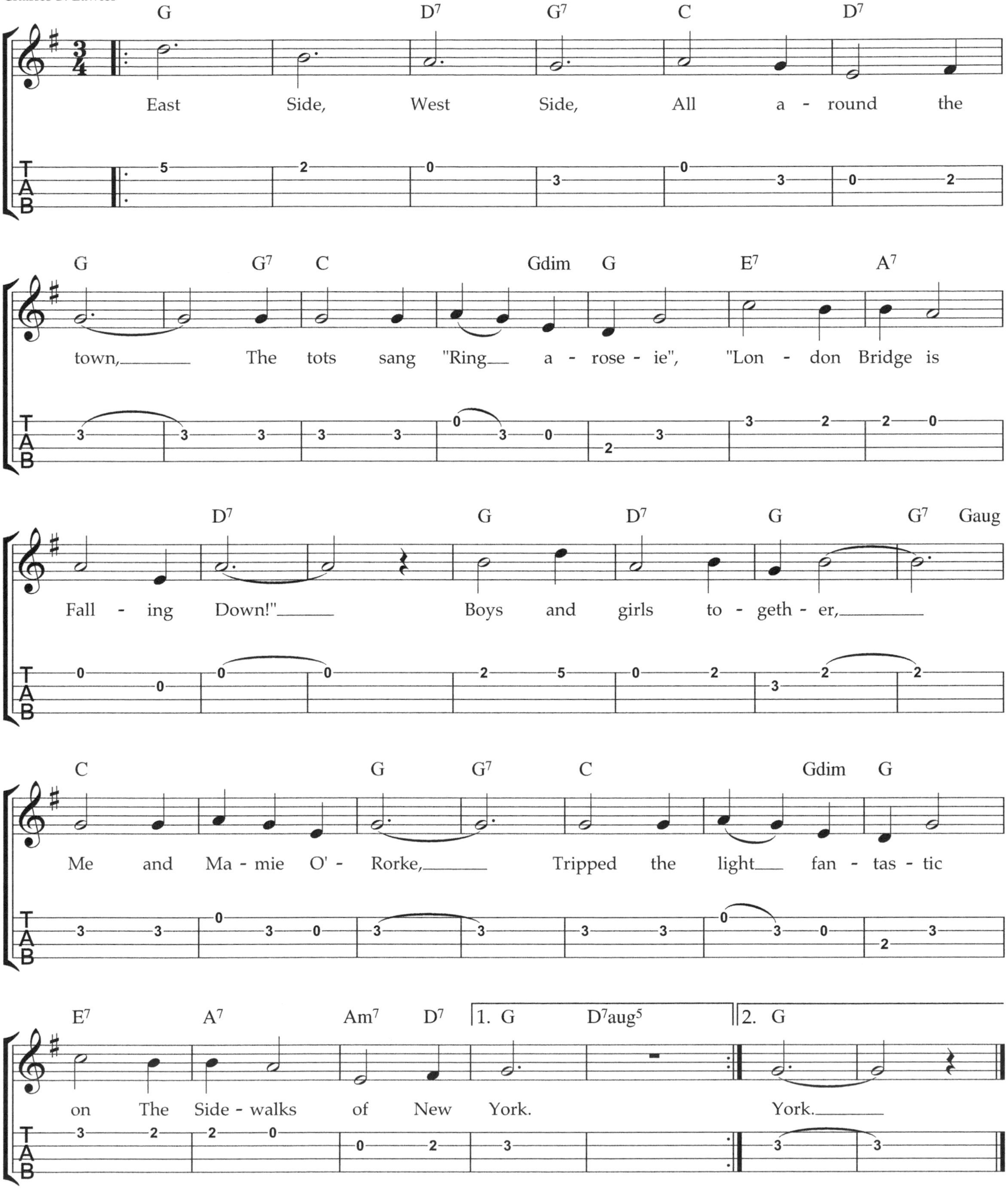
G D7 G7 C D7
East Side, West Side, All a - round the
G G7 C Gdim G E7 A7
town, The tots sang "Ring a - rose - ie", "Lon - don Bridge is
D7 G D7 G G7 Gaug
Fall - ing Down!" Boys and girls to - geth - er,
C G G7 C Gdim G
Me and Ma - mie O' - Rorke, Tripped the light fan - tas - tic
E7 A7 Am7 D7 1. G D7aug5 2. G
on The Side - walks of New York. York.
TAB

Spanish Is The Loving Tongue

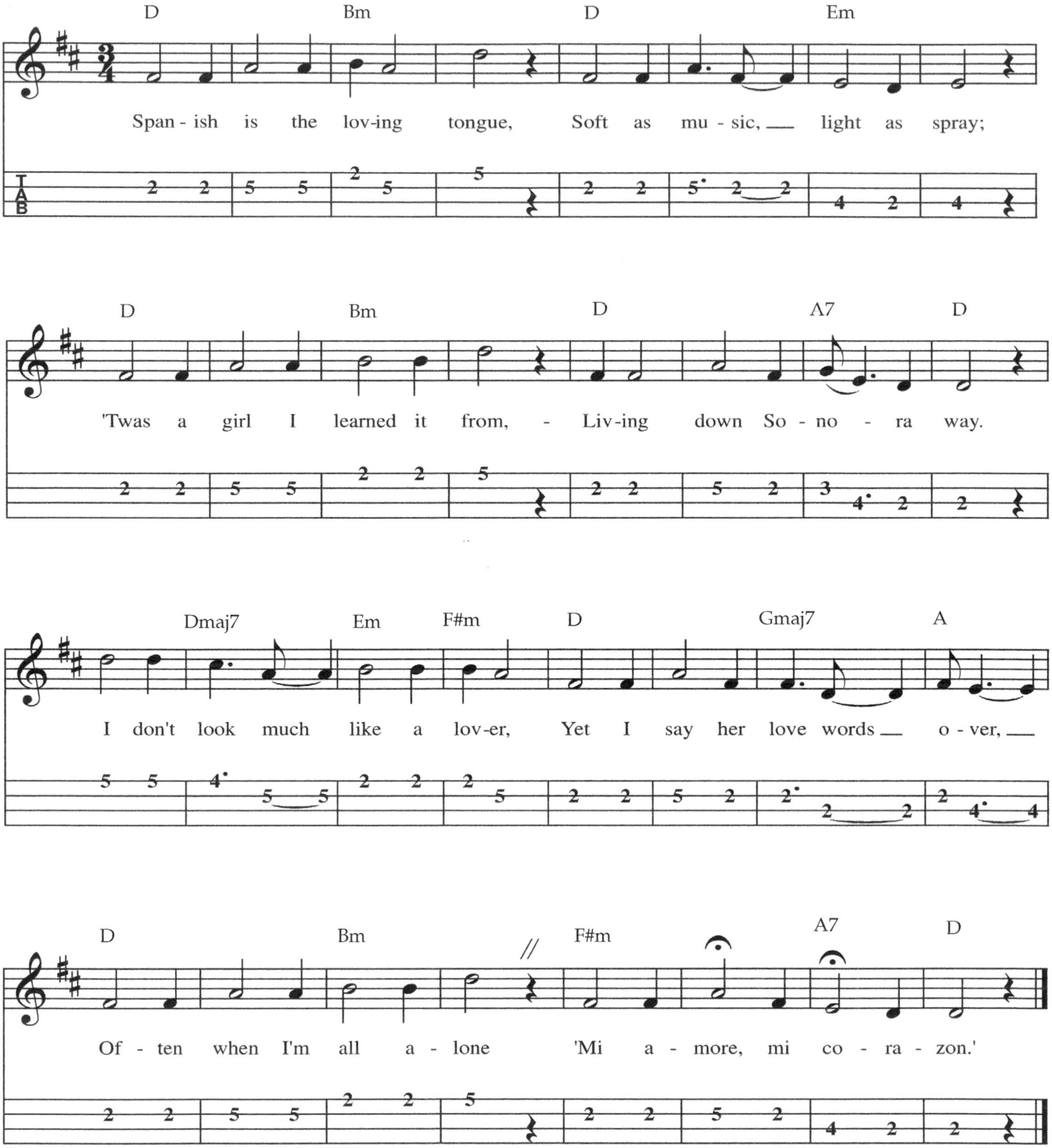
D Bm D Em
Span - ish is the lov-ing tongue, Soft as mu - sic, light as spray;
D Bm D A7 D
'Twas a girl I learned it from, - Liv-ing down So - no - ra way.
Dmaj7 Em F#m D Gmaj7 A
I don't look much like a lov-er, Yet I say her love words o - ver,
D Bm F#m A7 D
Of - ten when I'm all a - lone 'Mi a - more, mi co - ra - zon.'

Sweet Lei Lehua

Chas. E. King

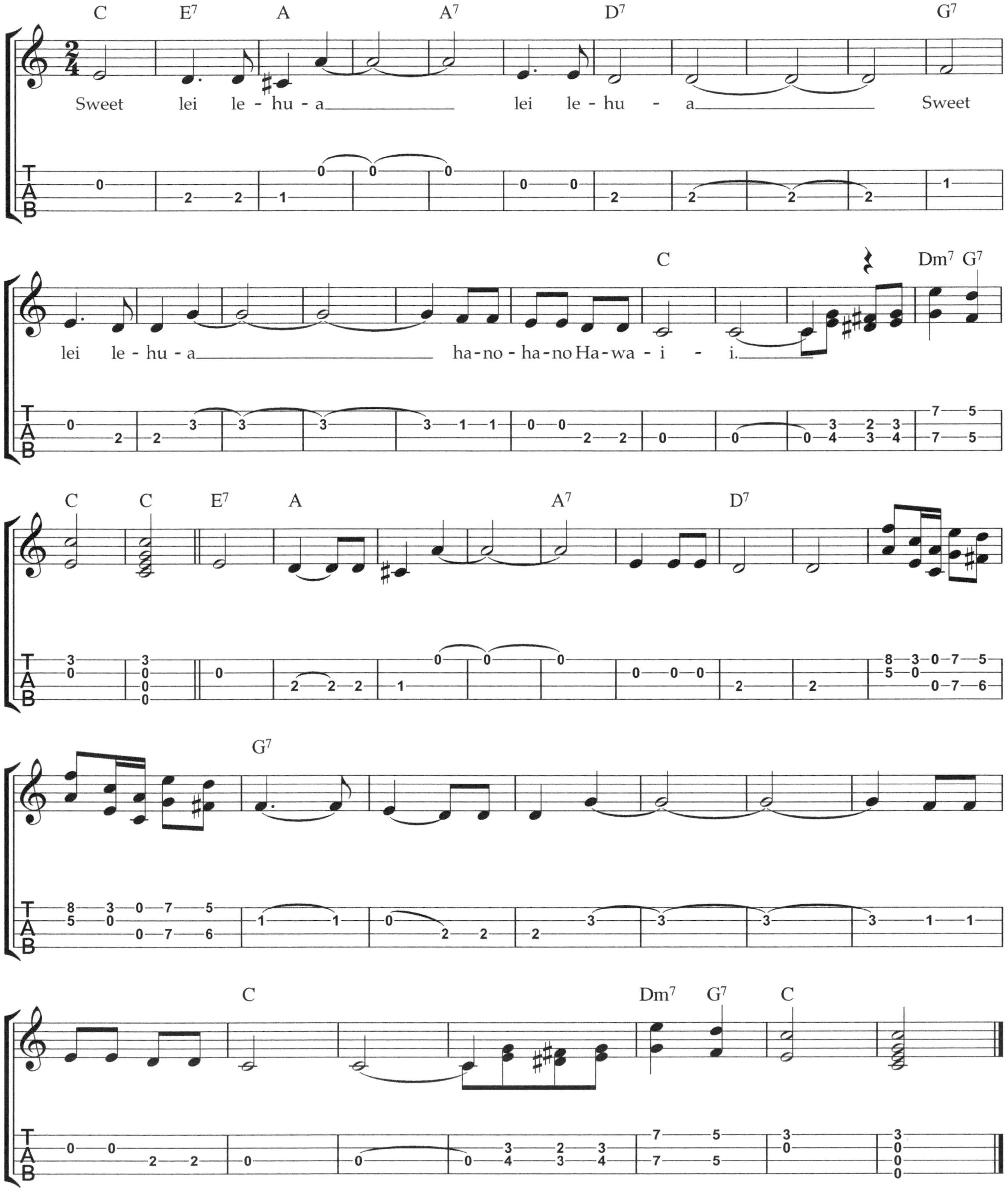
C E7 A A7 D7 G7
Sweet lei le - hu - a lei le - hu - a Sweet
C Dm7 G7
lei le - hu - a ha - no - ha - no Ha - wa - i - i.
C C E7 A A7 D7
G7
C Dm7 G7 C

Swingin' Down The Lane

Lyrics by
Gus Kahn

Music by
Isham Jones

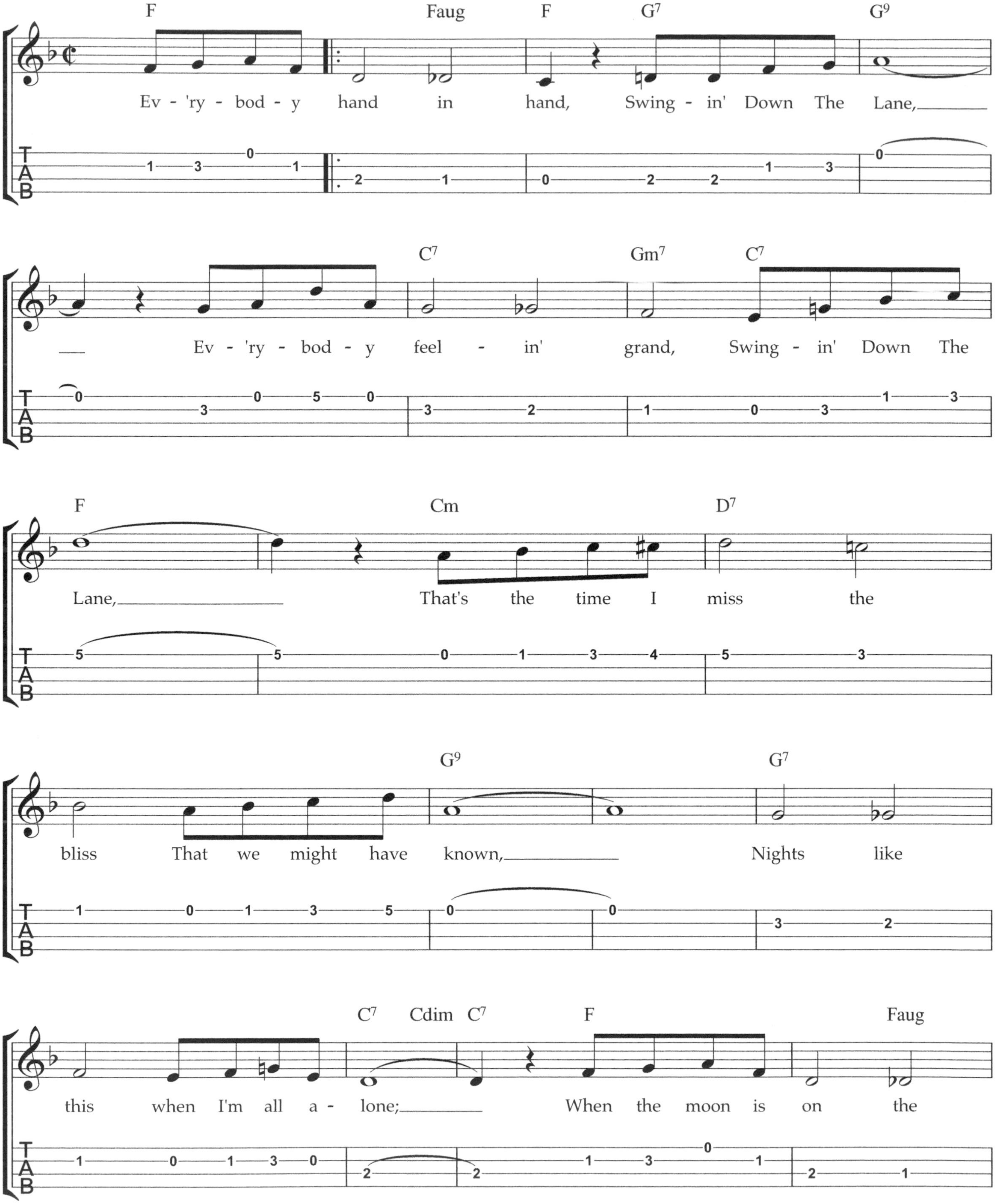
F Faug F G7 G9
Ev - 'ry - bod - y hand in hand, Swing - in' Down The Lane,
C7 Gm7 C7
Ev - 'ry - bod - y feel - in' grand, Swing - in' Down The
F Cm D7
Lane, That's the time I miss the
G9 G7
bliss That we might have known, Nights like
C7 Cdim C7 F Faug
this when I'm all a - lone; When the moon is on the

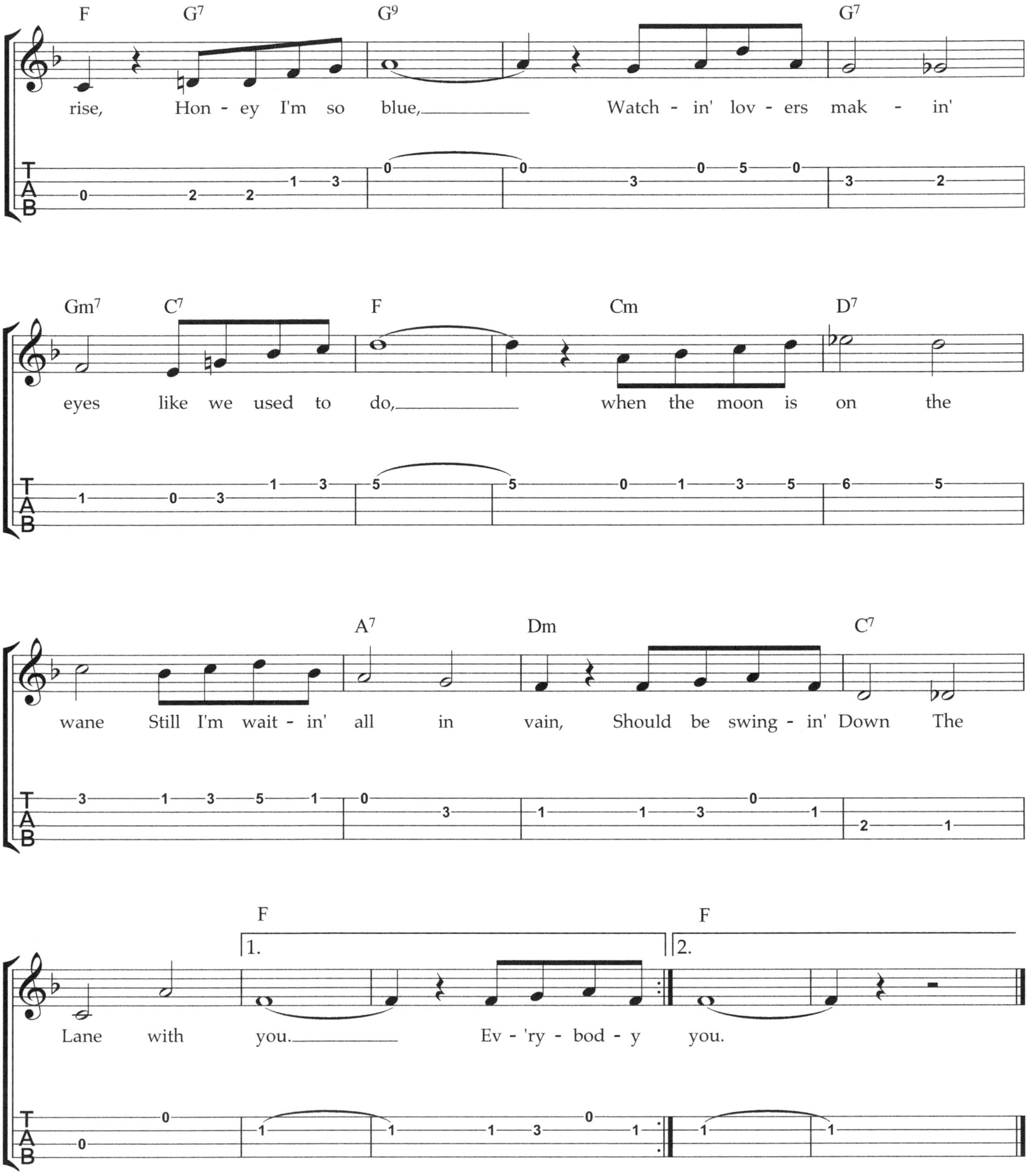
F G7 G9 G7
rise, Hon - ey I'm so blue, Watch - in' lov - ers mak - in'
Gm7 C7 F Cm D7
eyes like we used to do, when the moon is on the
A7 Dm C7
wane Still I'm wait - in' all in vain, Should be swing - in' Down The
F F
1. 2.
Lane with you. Ev - 'ry - bod - y you.

Ten Little Fingers And Ten Little Toes

Words by
Harry Pease and
Johnny White

Music by
Ira Schuster and
Ed. G. Nelson

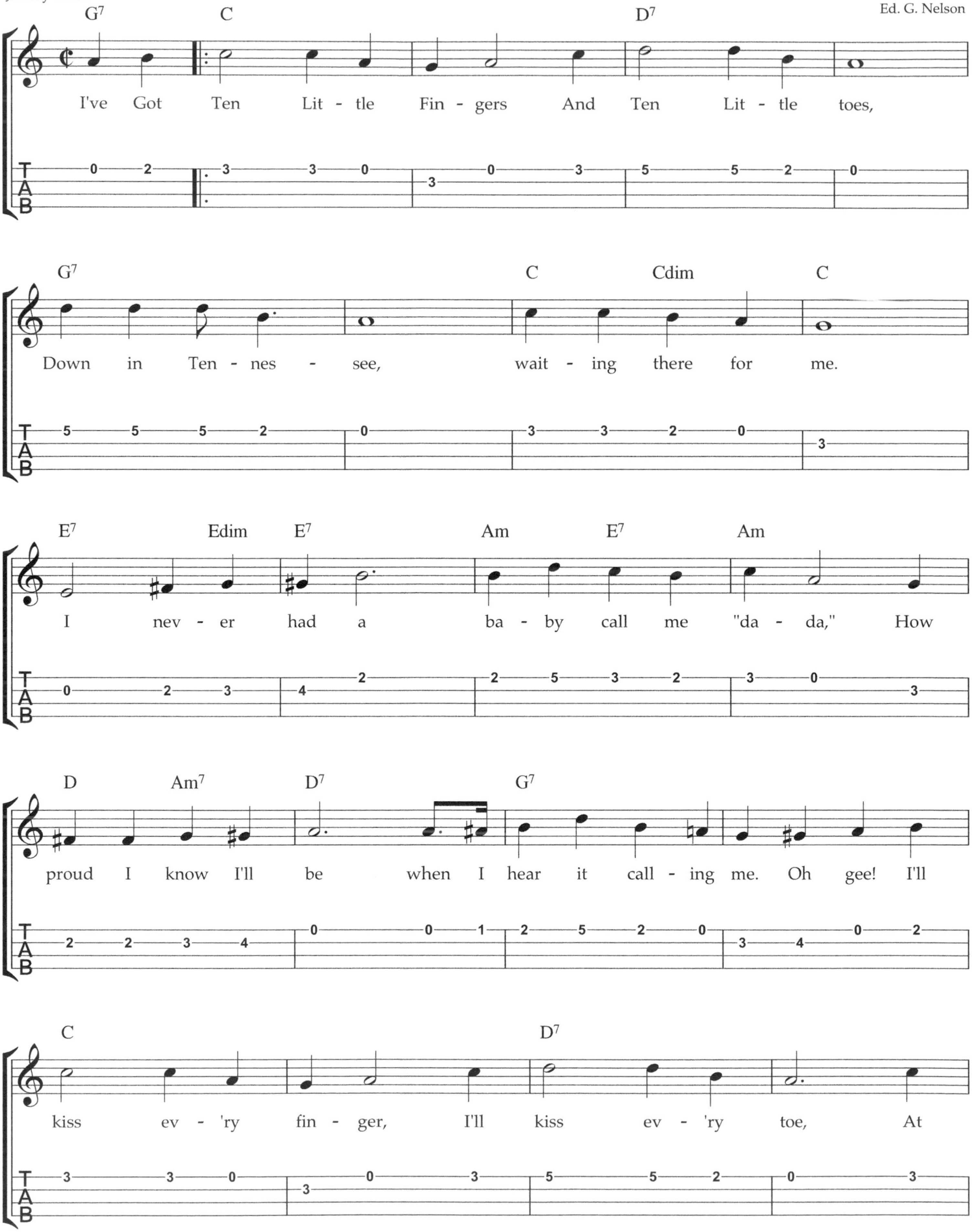
G7 C D7
I've Got Ten Lit - tle Fin - gers And Ten Lit - tle toes,
G7 C Cdim C
Down in Ten - nes - see, wait - ing there for me.
E7 Edim E7 Am E7 Am
I nev - er had a ba - by call me "da - da," How
D Am7 D7 G7
proud I know I'll be when I hear it call - ing me. Oh gee! I'll
C D7
kiss ev - 'ry fin - ger, I'll kiss ev - 'ry toe, At

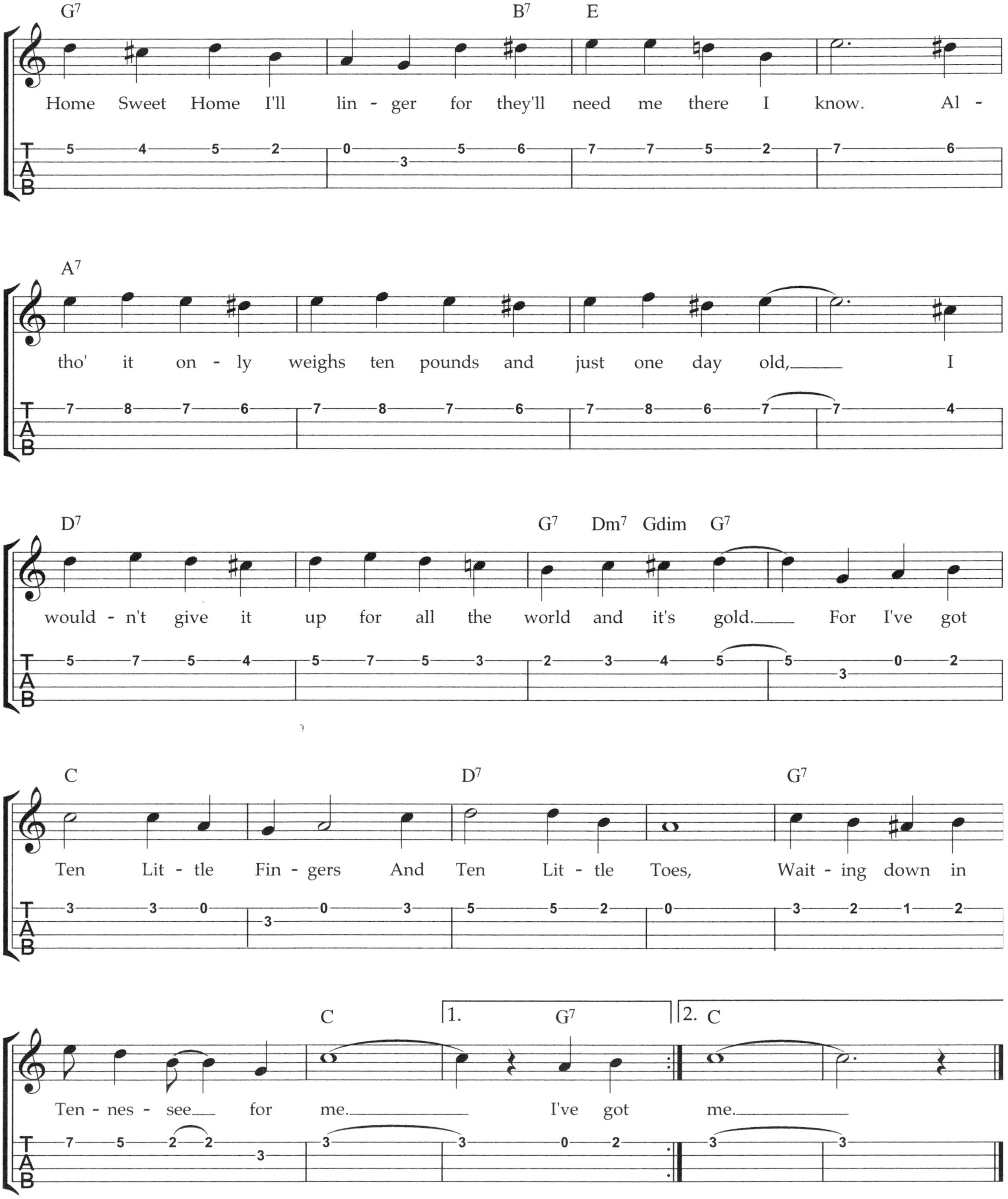
G7 B7 E
Home Sweet Home I'll lin - ger for they'll need me there I know. Al -
A7
tho' it on - ly weighs ten pounds and just one day old, I
D7 G7 Dm7 Gdim G7
would - n't give it up for all the world and it's gold. For I've got
C D7 G7
Ten Lit - tle Fin - gers And Ten Lit - tle Toes, Wait - ing down in
C 1. G7 2. C
Ten - nes - see for me. I've got me.

Toot, Toot, Tootsie!

by Gus Kahn,
Ernie Erdman
and Dan Russo

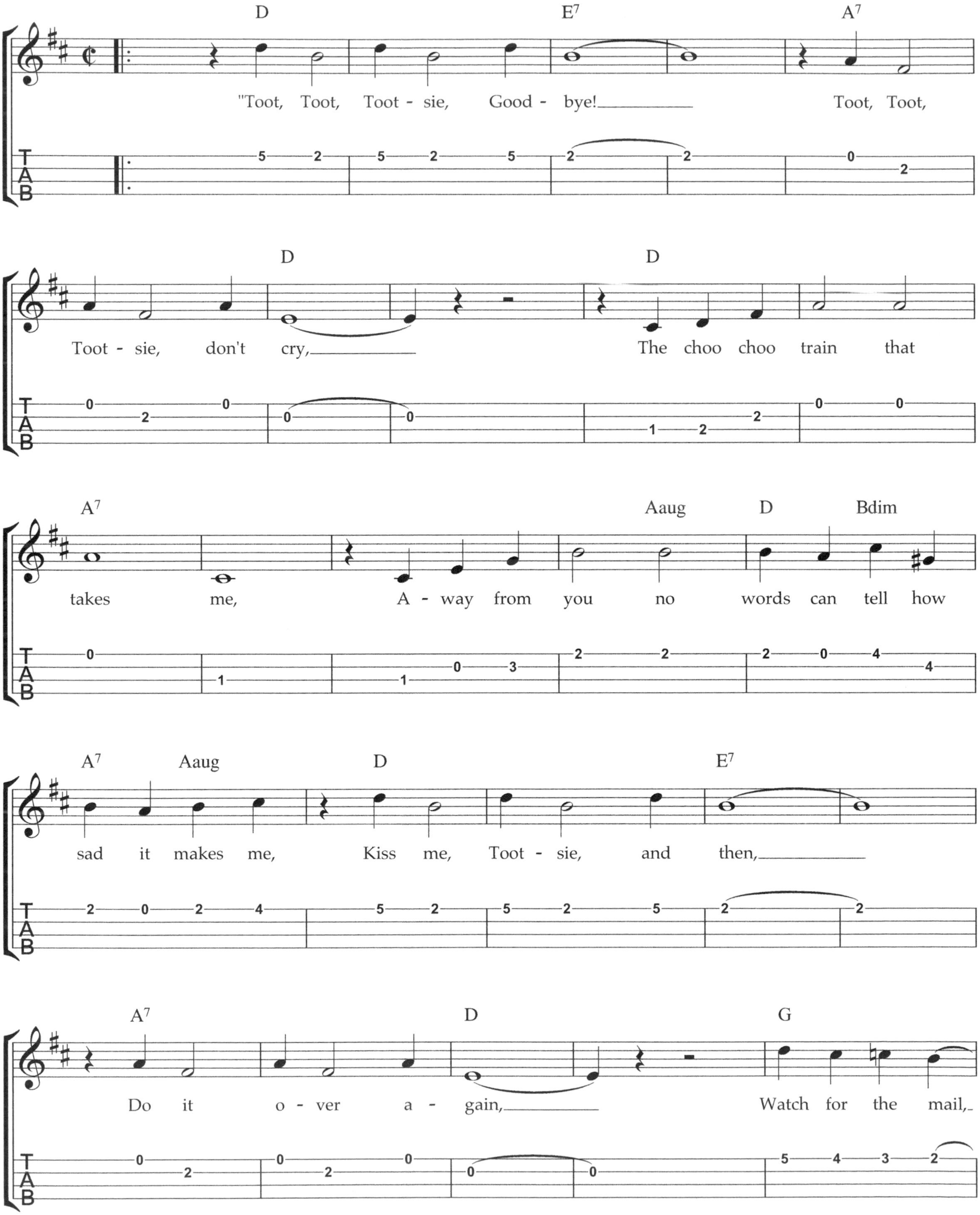
D E7 A7
"Toot, Toot, Toot - sie, Good - bye! Toot, Toot,
D D
Toot - sie, don't cry, The choo choo train that
A7 Aaug D Bdim
takes me, A - way from you no words can tell how
A7 Aaug D E7
sad it makes me, Kiss me, Toot - sie, and then,
A7 D G
Do it o - ver a - gain, Watch for the mail,
T
A
B

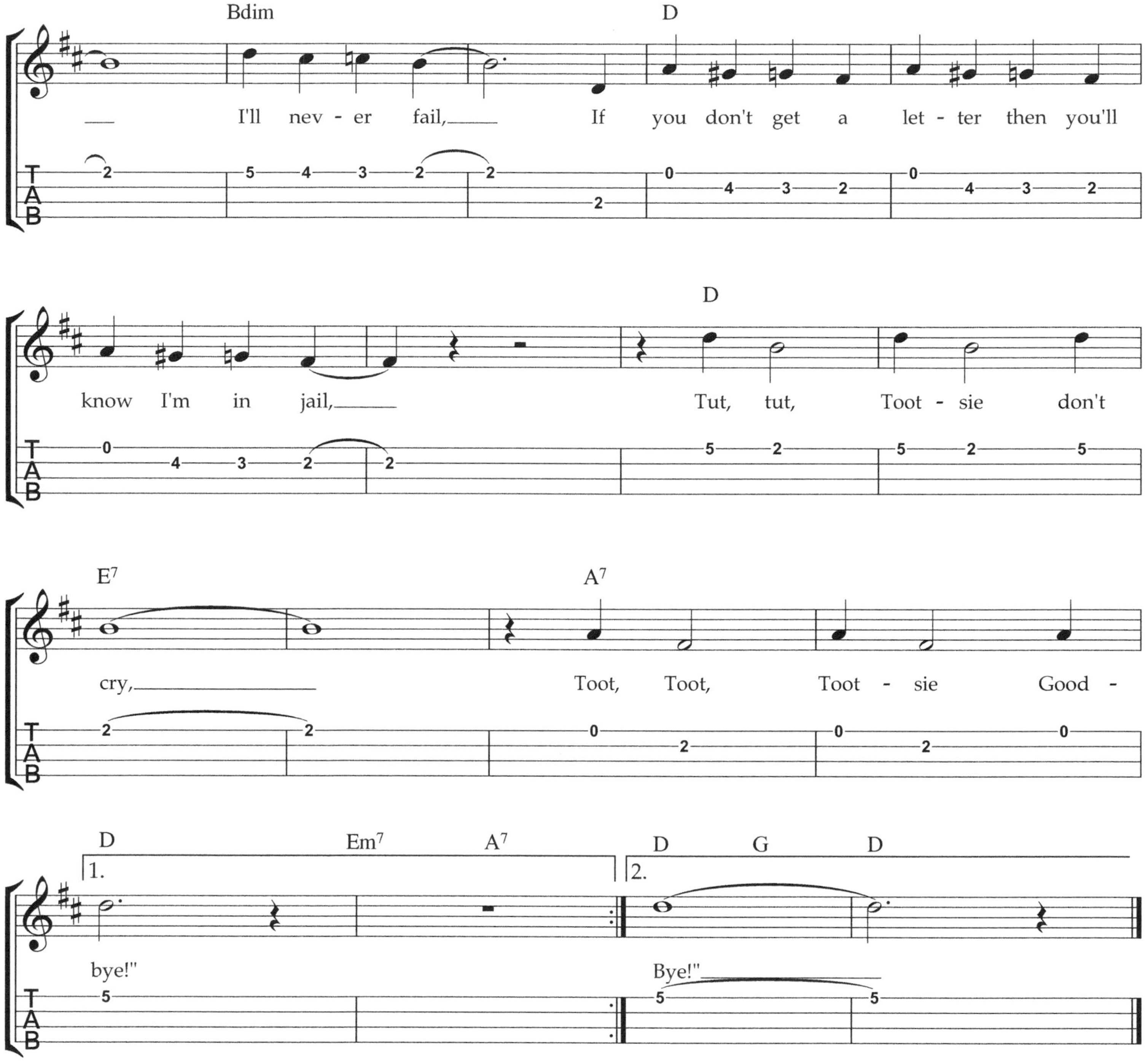
Bdim
D
I'll nev - er fail,
If you don't get a let - ter then you'll
know I'm in jail,
D
Tut, tut, Toot - sie don't
E7
A7
cry,
Toot, Toot, Toot - sie Good -
D
Em7
A7
D
G
D
1.
2.
bye!"
Bye!"

Under The Bamboo Tree

Words by
Bob Cole

Music by
Rosamond Johnson

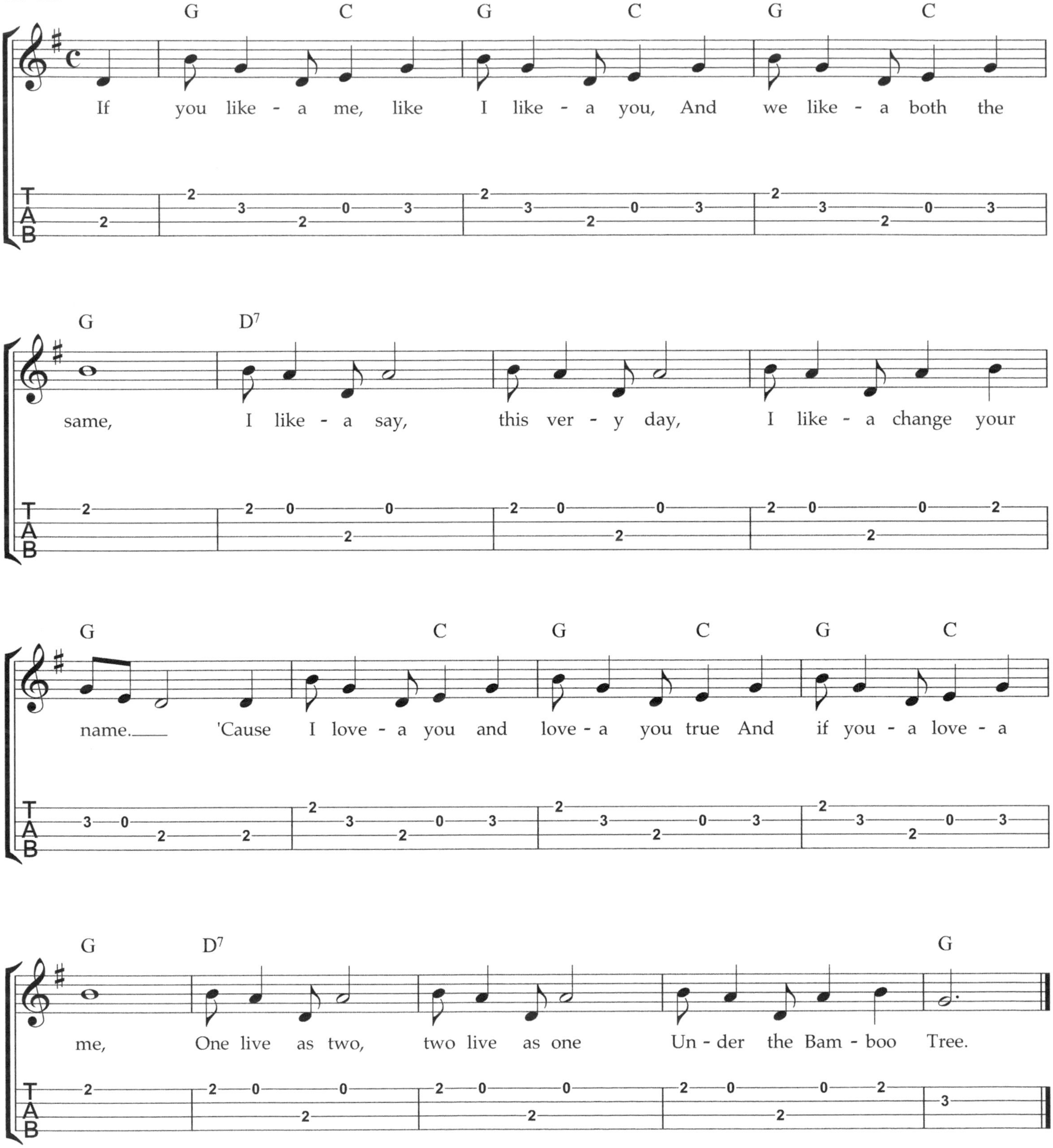
G C G C G C
If you like - a me, like I like - a you, And we like - a both the
G D7
same, I like - a say, this ver - y day, I like - a change your
G C G C G C
name.___ 'Cause I love - a you and love - a you true And if you - a love - a
G D7 G
me, One live as two, two live as one Un - der the Bam - boo Tree.

When Francis Dances With Me

Words by
Benny Ryan

Music by Violinsky

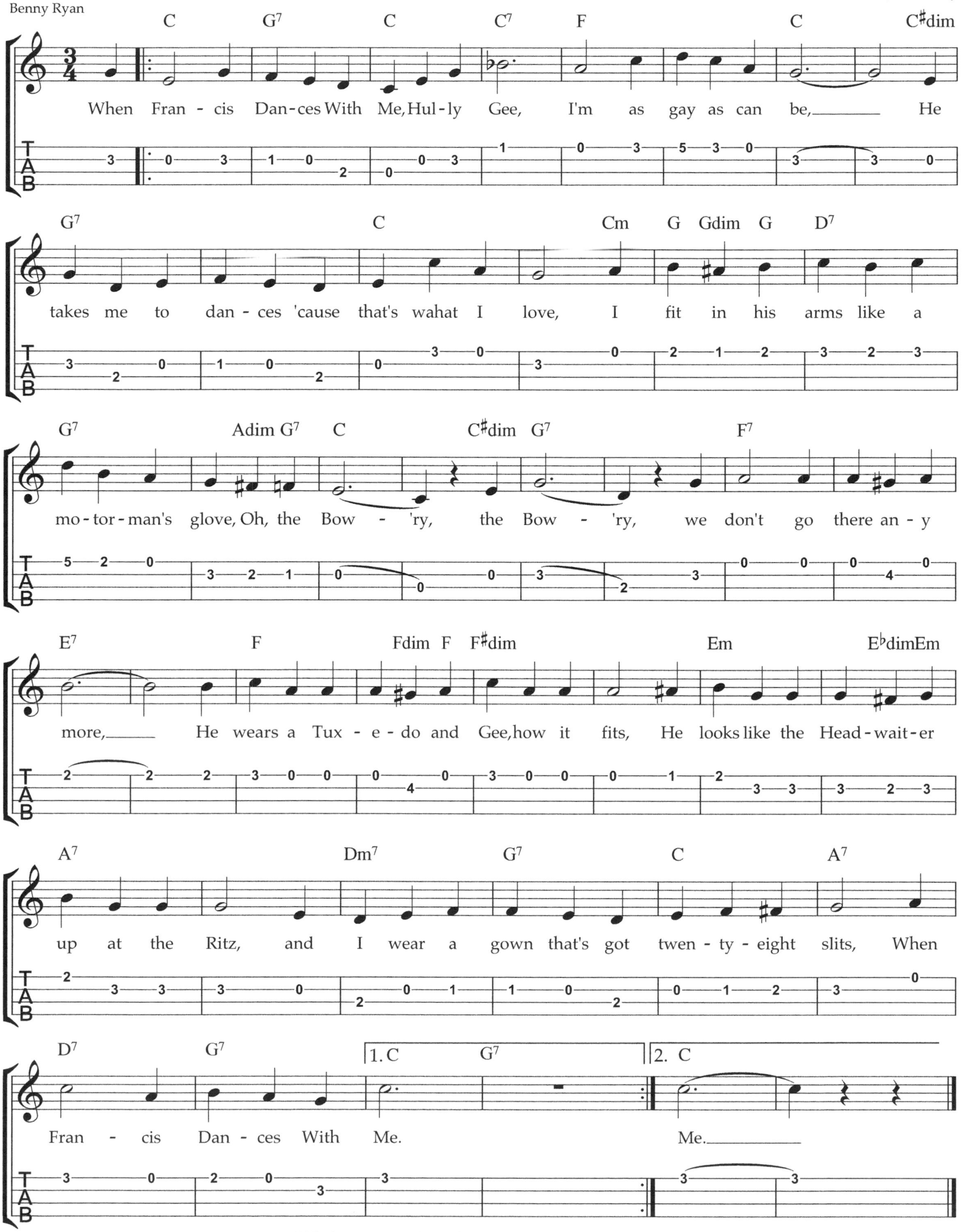
When Fran - cis Dan-ces With Me, Hul-ly Gee, I'm as gay as can be, He
takes me to dan - ces 'cause that's wahat I love, I fit in his arms like a
mo-tor-man's glove, Oh, the Bow - 'ry, the Bow - 'ry, we don't go there an - y
more, He wears a Tux - e - do and Gee, how it fits, He looks like the Head-wait-er
up at the Ritz, and I wear a gown that's got twen - ty - eight slits, When
Fran - cis Dan - ces With Me.
Me.

When You Wore A Tulip

Words by
Jack Mahoney

Music by
Percy Wenrich

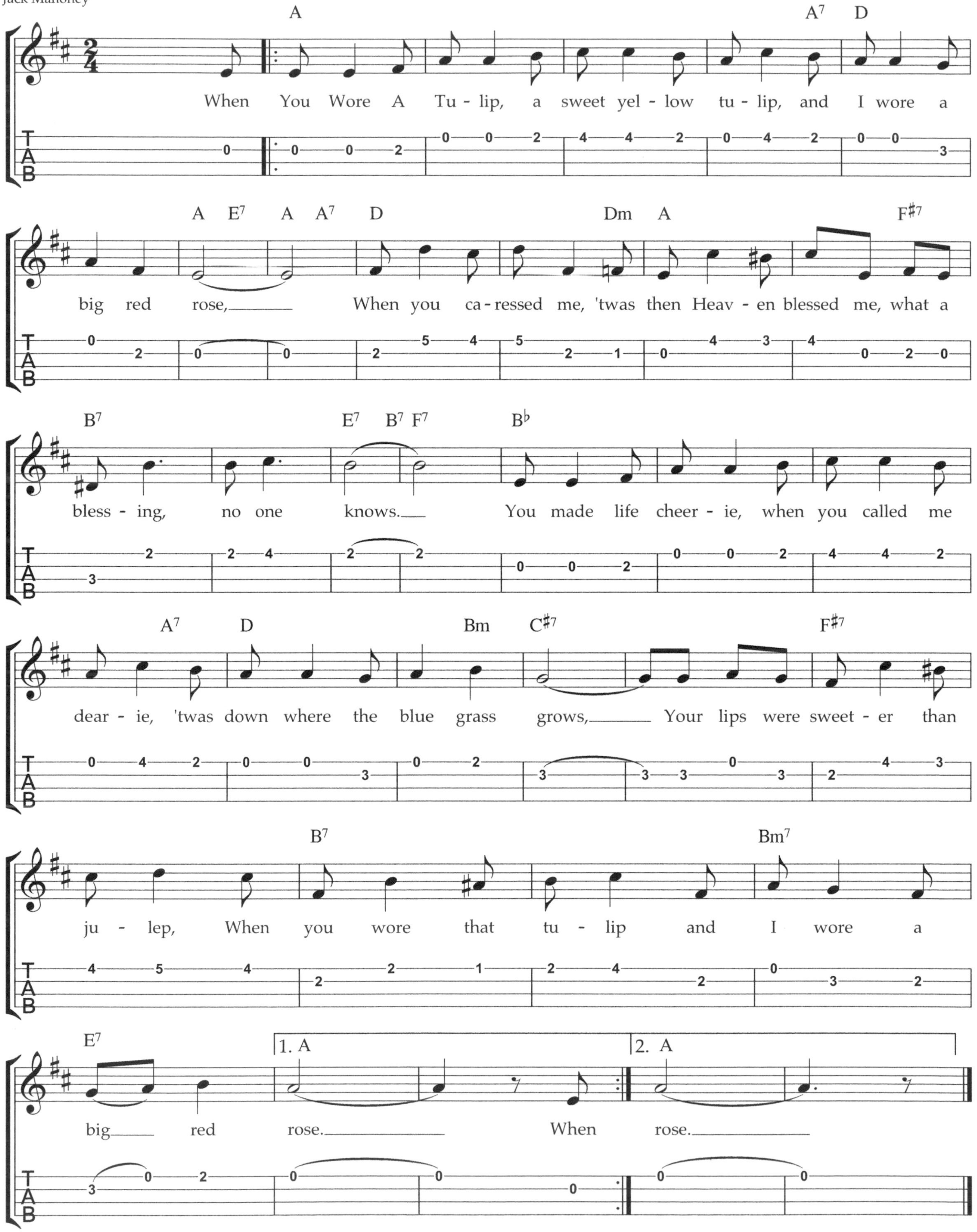
A A7 D
When You Wore A Tu - lip, a sweet yel - low tu - lip, and I wore a
A E7 A A7 D Dm A F#7
big red rose, When you ca - ressed me, 'twas then Heav - en blessed me, what a
B7 E7 B7 F7 B♭
bless - ing, no one knows. You made life cheer - ie, when you called me
A7 D Bm C#7 F#7
dear - ie, 'twas down where the blue grass grows, Your lips were sweet - er than
B7 Bm7
ju - lep, When you wore that tu - lip and I wore a
E7 1. A 2. A
big red rose. When rose.

Whispering

Word and Music by John Schonberge,
Richard Coburn and Vincent Rose

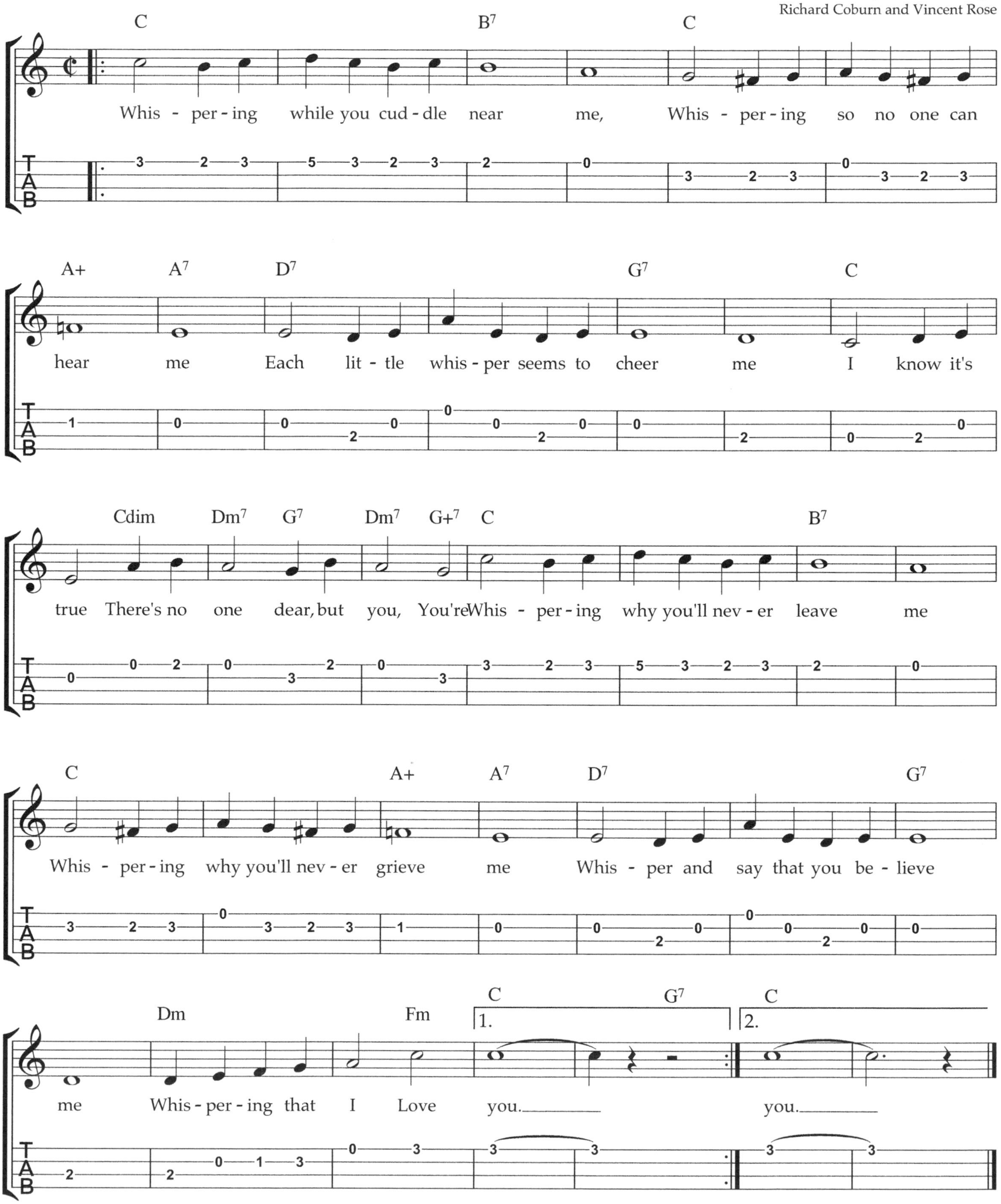
C B7 C
Whis - per - ing while you cud - dle near me, Whis - per - ing so no one can
A+ A7 D7 G7 C
hear me Each lit - tle whis - per seems to cheer me I know it's
Cdim Dm7 G7 Dm7 G+7 C B7
true There's no one dear, but you, You're Whis - per - ing why you'll nev - er leave me
C A+ A7 D7 G7
Whis - per - ing why you'll nev - er grieve me Whis - per and say that you be - lieve
Dm Fm C G7 C
1. 2.
me Whis - per - ing that I Love you. you.
T
A
B

You've Got To See Mamma Ev'ry Night

by Billy Rose
and Con Conrad

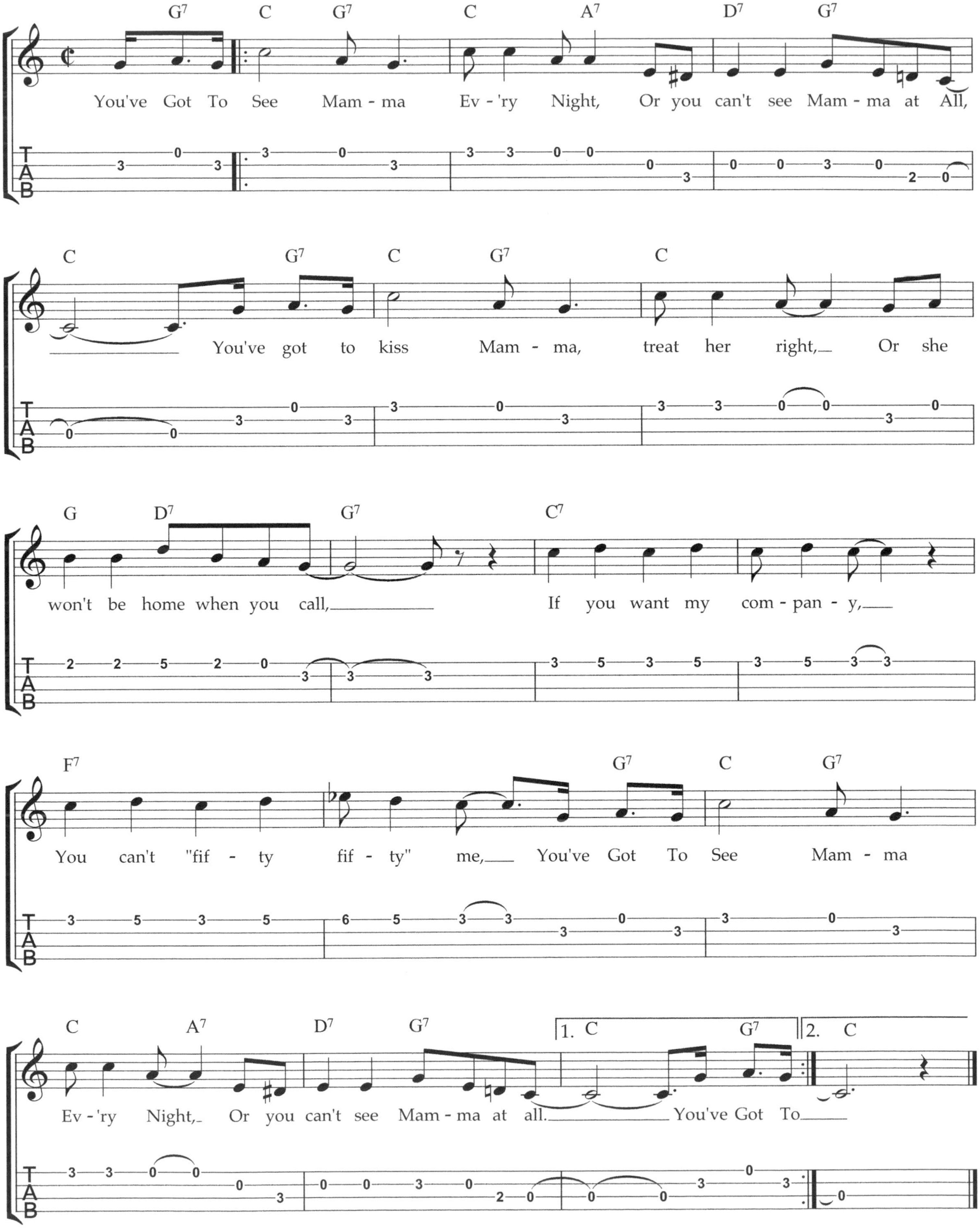
G7 C G7 C A7 D7 G7
You've Got To See Mam - ma Ev - 'ry Night, Or you can't see Mam - ma at All,
C G7 C G7 C
You've got to kiss Mam - ma, treat her right, Or she
G D7 G7 C7
won't be home when you call, If you want my com - pan - y,
F7 G7 C G7
You can't "fif - ty fif - ty" me, You've Got To See Mam - ma
C A7 D7 G7 1. C G7 2. C
Ev - 'ry Night, Or you can't see Mam - ma at all. You've Got To
T
A
B